Agile Marketing in a F~~~~ ~

Strategies for A~

K.Manoj

ISBN NO : 978-93-5868-302-8

Table of content

Chapter 1: Understanding the Need for Agile Marketing.

Recognizing Agile Marketing's Need

In the dynamic and constantly evolving corporate environment of today, conventional marketing approaches can prove inadequate for satisfying the needs of contemporary consumers and maintaining a competitive edge. Agile marketing, a dynamic and adaptable strategy that enables businesses to quickly adjust to shifting consumer preferences and market situations, has become increasingly necessary as a result. This essay will explore the idea of agile marketing, its significance, its guiding principles, and how it may support companies in thriving in a world that is becoming more digital and customer-focused.

Similar to its counterpart in software development, agile marketing is founded on the Agile Manifesto. It places a strong emphasis on adaptability, teamwork, and customer-centricity with the ultimate goal of producing results rapidly and effectively. Agile marketing emphasizes being responsive, iterative, and adaptive in contrast to traditional marketing strategies, which can need long-term strategy and implementation.

The digital revolution that has altered the marketing environment is one of the main factors necessitating agile marketing. The emergence of digital technologies, social media, and the internet has drastically changed how customers engage with brands. They want instantaneous responses, tailored experiences, and real-time involvement since information is readily available to them. Conventional marketing techniques are frequently inadequate to satisfy these needs.

Furthermore, marketers must move quickly and decisively based on data due to the massive amount of data generated by internet interactions. Data and analytics are essential for comprehending customer behavior and market trends in an agile marketing strategy. These insights can be used by marketers to quickly adjust their campaigns and plans.

The dynamic nature of consumer tastes necessitates quick adaptation and a willingness to change quickly in order to remain relevant. This is the sweet spot for agile marketing. Rather than adhering to inflexible strategies that can become antiquated, agile marketing teams are flexible enough to modify their emphasis, tactics, and messaging as circumstances demand.

Key ideas that highlight the necessity of agile marketing are as follows:

Quick Reaction to Market Changes: Marketing strategies can easily become outmoded or irrelevant in today's world when news and trends circulate swiftly via social media and other digital platforms. Teams using agile marketing are able to react quickly to shifting market conditions, which keeps their messaging relevant and powerful.

Iterative improvement is the foundation of agile marketing, which emphasizes continuous improvement. Teams may determine what works and what doesn't in marketing initiatives by continuously testing and evaluating them. This allows them to make necessary adjustments to maximize their plans. Agile marketing is known for its "test and learn" methodology.

Agile marketing centers all choices around the needs and wants of the customer. Organizations can adjust their marketing tactics to match the unique requirements and preferences of their target audience by continuously collecting and evaluating customer data.

Cooperation and Cross-Functionality: Agile marketing encourages cross-functional cooperation by dismantling departmental silos. This makes it possible for marketing to take a more integrated and holistic approach, with teams cooperating to accomplish shared objectives.

Accountability and Transparency: Agile marketing places a strong emphasis on these two concepts. Teams accept accountability for their actions and are transparent about their difficulties and progress. This transparent culture promotes trust as well as ongoing development.

Data-Driven Decision-Making: Agile marketing relies heavily on data. To monitor the effect of their work and make modifications based on real-time insights, teams rely on data and analytics to make well-informed decisions.

Agile marketing teams usually use a variety of techniques and procedures to put these ideas into action. The Scrum framework, which was taken from Agile software development, is one of the most widely used. Work is arranged using Scrum into brief, time-boxed iterations known as "sprints." Usually lasting between two and four weeks, each sprint produces a potentially shippable product increment. This could refer to a particular marketing campaign, piece of information, or characteristic of a product.

Every sprint involves the team organizing, carrying out, and assessing their work. They gather periodically for "stand-up" sessions to discuss progress, handle difficulties, and plan the next steps. Marketing teams may adapt their strategies, be more responsive, and gain knowledge from the results of each sprint by using this iterative strategy.

Another agile marketing framework is Kanban. Its main objectives are to prioritize tasks, visualize the work that is being done, and continuously enhance workflows. Groups monitor every task's progress using a Kanban board, which allows them to move it through various stages like "To-Do," "In Progress," and "Done." Teams can manage their work more effectively and transparently with the use of this technique.

Agile marketing can help both B2B and B2C companies in a variety of sectors; it is not restricted to any one industry or kind of company. Actually, both established businesses and startups are using it more and more. Agile marketing is a flexible and scalable strategy that works well for businesses of all sizes.

Agile marketing provides a quick and affordable means for new businesses to connect with their target market. Startups must be able to quickly adjust their course in reaction to feedback from the market because they frequently have little funding and few resources. Without spending a fortune, agile marketing enables them to test their hypotheses, modify their plans, and increase brand recognition.

On the other hand, established businesses can find that agile marketing is necessary to maintain their competitiveness in the quickly evolving market of today. These companies frequently have intricate procedures and structures, which can impede decision-making and implementation. Agile marketing can assist companies in becoming more responsive and nimble, which will allow them to introduce new goods or campaigns more rapidly and more successfully.

Agile marketing's capacity to promote innovation is one of its most noteworthy advantages. Conventional marketing strategies frequently take a formulaic, risk-averse approach, depending on what has already proven effective. Agile marketing, on the other hand, values innovation and trial and error. Teams are free to experiment with novel concepts and methods, taking lessons from both their achievements and setbacks. A brand can differentiate itself from the competition by using innovative ideas and campaigns that result from this innovative culture.

There are difficulties with agile marketing. A change in the organization's culture is necessary for this strategy to be implemented. It demands a dedication to openness, cooperation, and ongoing education. It can also necessitate training marketing personnel and investing in new technology. Furthermore, not every kind of marketing activity can profit from agile marketing; some initiatives or campaigns can still be better off with conventional planning and execution.

The following actions must be taken by firms in order to successfully adopt agile marketing:

Leadership Buy-In: To guarantee that the required resources and cultural shifts are in place, agile marketing needs the backing of the highest levels of the organization.

Training and Education: Agile principles and practices should be taught to marketing teams. This entails being aware of ideas like data-driven decision-making, stand-up meetings, and sprints.

Create cross-functional teams by assembling people with a range of backgrounds and specialties. This encourages teamwork and the capacity to provide comprehensive marketing solutions.

Data-Driven Approach: To make wise judgments and assess the success of marketing initiatives, spend money on analytics tools and collect pertinent data.

Pilot Projects: To test the agile marketing strategy, begin with pilot projects. Refine the process by taking lessons from these early encounters.

Encourage a culture of continuous improvement where teams evaluate their work on a regular basis and look for methods to improve its effectiveness and efficiency.

In summary, the ever-evolving demands of consumers, the emergence of digital technology, and the quickly changing corporate landscape all contribute to the need for agile marketing. In response to these difficulties, agile marketing emerged as a flexible and adaptable method of marketing that is based on the ideas of customer-centricity, teamwork, and data-driven decision-making. This strategy can accelerate time-to-market, stimulate innovation, and improve consumer engagement for both new and established businesses. Organizations must be dedicated to changing their culture, make technological and training investments, and consistently enhance their operations if they hope to thrive with agile marketing. Agility is a need in the fast-paced world of today, not just a competitive advantage.

The Evolution of Marketing: From Traditional to Agile.

The Marketing Evolution: From Conventional to Agile

From its traditional beginnings to its current state of agility and adaptability, marketing has gone a long way. The dynamic shifts in consumer behavior, technology breakthroughs, and corporate practices across time are reflected in the evolution of marketing. This essay will examine the evolution of marketing, from its inception to the rise of agile marketing, and the major forces behind this change.

Conventional Marketing: Formerly known as "outbound marketing," traditional marketing was the most common strategy. It included a number of tactics meant to reach a wide audience with marketing messages. These tactics made use of print, radio, television, billboards, and direct mail, among other mass media outlets. Among the essential elements of conventional marketing were:

A. Mass Advertising: In the past, marketing relied heavily on developing messages that were compelling and disseminating them to a large audience. This strategy was predicated on the idea that a high volume of impressions would eventually result in conversions.

B. Protracted Planning Cycles: Conventional marketing initiatives frequently necessitated protracted planning and preparation. As a result, marketing messages and tactics were fixed for long stretches of time, making it difficult to adjust to shifting market conditions.

C. Limited Audience Targeting: Precise targeting was not possible with mass media. Instead of having access to real-time data on customer behavior and preferences, marketers had to rely on demographics and assumptions about their target audience.

C. Innovation: Agile marketing promotes experimentation and creativity, which in turn stimulates innovation. Teams are free to experiment with novel concepts and methods, taking lessons from both their achievements and setbacks. A brand can differentiate itself from the competition by using innovative ideas and campaigns that result from this innovative culture.

Problems and Things to Think About: Agile marketing has many benefits, but there are drawbacks as well. For agile marketing to be implemented successfully, organizations must take into account following factors:

A. Organizational Culture transformation: Agile marketing necessitates an organizational culture transformation. It demands a dedication to openness, cooperation, and ongoing education.

B. Education and Training: Agile approaches and principles must be taught to marketing teams. This entails being aware of ideas like data-driven decision-making, stand-up meetings, and sprints.

C. Cross-Functional Teams: Agile marketing requires the formation of cross-functional teams with a variety of talents and specialties. This encourages teamwork and the capacity to provide comprehensive marketing solutions.

D. Data-Driven Approach: In order to make wise decisions and assess the success of marketing initiatives, businesses must invest in analytics tools and collect pertinent data.

E. Pilot initiatives: Organizations can test the agile marketing approach by beginning with pilot initiatives. These early encounters offer insightful information and aid in process improvement.

F. Continuous Improvement: The success of agile marketing depends on fostering a culture of continuous improvement, where teams constantly evaluate their work and look for methods to make it more effective and efficient.

In conclusion, the shift in marketing from traditional to agile is a reflection of how company processes, technology, and customer behavior are evolving. While digital marketing made use of data-driven tactics and the internet, conventional marketing depended on mass advertising through traditional media channels. However, agile marketing emerged as a response to the demand for flexibility, adaptability, and customer-centricity.

Customer-centricity, flexibility in real-time, teamwork, data-driven decision-making, iterative improvement, accountability, and openness are the hallmarks of agile marketing. It uses techniques like as Scrum, Kanban, and Lean to implement these ideas. Agile marketing promotes innovation and facilitates quicker responses to market dynamics, which benefits both startups and established businesses. It is not restricted to any one industry or type of company.

Organizations that want to succeed with agile marketing must make a culture shift commitment, make technology and training investments, and maintain ongoing process improvement. Agility is not just a competitive advantage in today's fast-paced world, but it is also a need for marketers who want to succeed in a constantly changing environment.

The Fast-Paced Business Landscape: Challenges and Opportunities.

The Advancing Business Environment: Difficulties and Possibilities

The corporate environment is fast-paced and constantly changing in the digital age. Technology developments, alterations in customer behavior, and upheavals in the global economy have created a dynamic environment in which businesses must continually adapt in order to survive and prosper. There are opportunities and problems in this fast-paced corporate environment that must be carefully navigated. We shall examine the main difficulties and chances brought about by the quick changes in the current business environment in this article.

Difficulties in the Rapidly Changing Business Environment:

Technological Disruption: In the quick-paced world of business, technology can be both a benefit and a liability. On the one hand, it makes productivity, creativity, and the development of new market prospects possible. However, it also presents a continuous challenge because companies need to keep up with the latest technology developments and make necessary investments. People who don't adapt can easily become outdated.

For example, the emergence of automation, the Internet of Things (IoT), and artificial intelligence (AI) has completely changed the industrial, healthcare, and finance sectors. Businesses who do not adopt these technologies run the danger of slipping behind their rivals.

Reduced Product Lifecycles: Shorter product lifecycles are a result of the quick speed at which technology is developing. For example, consumer electronics age out of style in a few months, so businesses have to release new models on a regular basis. This may put a burden on available resources and make it difficult to recover R&D expenditures.

Fierce Competition: The low entry barriers brought forth by e-commerce and digital platforms have made many businesses more competitive. Startups have the ability to swiftly enter a market and unseat incumbents. To be competitive in this market, businesses need to constantly innovate, enhance client experiences, and set themselves apart.

Information Overload: There is an excessive volume of data and information produced by the quick-paced business environment. Companies may experience decision paralysis as a result of their inability to handle and interpret this data. Businesses need to build strong data analytics and interpretation skills if they want to prosper.

Changing Consumer Behavior: New technologies, societal changes, and changing expectations all have an impact on the ever-evolving behavior of consumers. Companies must be aware of these developments and modify their product and marketing plans as necessary. If this isn't done, consumers may stop being interested in the goods and services.

Cybersecurity Risks: As technology develops, so do cybercriminals' resources. Data breaches, ransomware attacks, and identity theft are just a few examples of the increasingly complex and common cybersecurity dangers. Businesses now place a high premium on safeguarding confidential information and guaranteeing the security of digital assets.

Supply Chain Disruptions: Natural disasters, geopolitical upheavals, and economic swings can all cause disruptions to global supply systems. There may be production delays, higher expenses, and even shortages as a result of these interruptions. In order to alleviate these difficulties, businesses need to create robust and adaptable supply chain plans.

Possibilities in the Quick-Changing Business Environment:

Innovation and Disruption: There are unmatched opportunities for both in the fast-paced commercial environment. Businesses have the opportunity to either dominate current markets or open up new ones if they can recognize rising trends, technologies, and client needs. The emergence of electric vehicles, the sharing economy, and the digital revolution in conventional industries are a few instances.

Global Reach: Businesses may now more easily reach markets throughout the world thanks to digital technologies. It is possible for small and medium-sized businesses to grow their clientele without having to establish physical presence in several places. This makes it possible to diversify and become less reliant on a particular market.

Agile Decision-Making: Organizations must create agile decision-making procedures if they are to succeed in a fast-paced setting. This calls for the capacity to evaluate circumstances fast, compile pertinent information, and come to well-informed conclusions. Agile decision-making enables businesses to take advantage of opportunities and overcome obstacles more skillfully.

Personalization: Businesses may provide their clients with highly tailored experiences thanks to the plethora of data and technology available to them. Increased revenue and brand recognition can result from personalization, which can also improve consumer loyalty and engagement. Businesses that use personalization well can obtain a competitive advantage.

Digital Marketing: Businesses now have strong tools at their disposal to connect and interact with their target audience thanks to the shift to digital marketing. Cost-effective and quantifiable methods of connecting with clients are provided via social media, influencer marketing, online advertising, and content marketing.

Data-Driven Insights: Businesses may benefit greatly from the massive amount of data generated in the digital age. Businesses may optimize their operations, make well-informed decisions, and create more successful marketing campaigns by utilizing data analytics and insights.

E-commerce: E-commerce has revolutionized the way companies offer goods and services. Businesses may reach consumers around-the-clock, cut expenses, and access international markets with the appropriate strategy. Additionally, e-commerce platforms have made it simpler for smaller companies to take on more established, larger competitors.

Flexible Work Environments: Companies are now able to access a wider talent pool and cut expenses related to office space thanks to the growing popularity of remote work and flexible work arrangements. Employees' work-life balance may be enhanced by this flexibility, which may also encourage a more inclusive and diverse staff.

Techniques for Succeeding in the Rapidly Changing Business Environment:

Constant Learning and Adaptation: A dedication to constant learning and adaptation is essential for success in today's fast-paced corporate environment. Employers must promote an innovative culture and urge staff members to keep abreast of market developments and new technological advancements.

Digital Transformation: It's imperative to embrace this change. Businesses should evaluate their digital capabilities and make investments in technology that improves their capacity for change, consumer interaction, and operational efficiency.

Customer-Centricity: It's imperative to give this top priority. Companies should actively seek out consumer input, keep an eye on their preferences and actions, and utilize this data to enhance their offerings.

Cooperation: It is crucial to collaborate with partners outside the company as well as within it. Cross-functional teams can foster creativity and make sure that every facet of the company is in line with the rapidly shifting demands of the market.

Risk management: In a fast-paced work environment, effective risk management is essential. Companies can lessen their vulnerability to market volatility by diversifying their revenue streams, creating backup plans, and routinely assessing risks.

Agility and Adaptability: Businesses should create agile procedures that enable them to quickly shift course and modify their plans as conditions warrant. This calls for adaptable decision-making, regular evaluations, and the capacity to change direction when called for.

Talent Development: Attracting and keeping top talent requires a significant investment in talent development. Companies should guarantee that employees have the skills necessary to succeed in the rapidly changing business environment by offering opportunities for growth and continual training.

Data Security: Businesses should give cybersecurity a priority in light of the growing risks to data security. This entails putting strong security measures in place, educating staff members about best practices, and routinely testing and upgrading security protocols.

In conclusion, businesses have both possibilities and problems in the rapidly evolving business environment. Adapting to the difficulties of rapid technology innovation, severe rivalry, and altering customer behavior requires effective tactics for success. However, opportunities for growth and prosperity are presented by the possibility for innovation, global reach, agile decision-making, personalization, and digital marketing.

Businesses need to promote customer-centricity, embrace teamwork, invest in digital transformation, cultivate a culture of continuous learning, manage risks, and stay flexible and nimble in order to succeed in this ever-changing market. An unrelenting commitment to development and the capacity to grasp possibilities as they present themselves while overcoming obstacles along the way are prerequisites for success in the fast-paced corporate environment.

The Concept of Agile Marketing: What It Is and What It Isn't.

Agile Marketing: An Overview of What It Is and Is Not

The term "agile marketing" has become increasingly popular in recent years. It signifies a change in marketing tactics and procedures, reflecting the Agile Manifesto's initial ideas, which were created for the software development industry. Nonetheless, agile marketing is sometimes misinterpreted or confused with other marketing strategies. To shed light on the essential traits and tenets of agile marketing, we shall examine what agile marketing is in this essay as well as—perhaps more importantly—what it isn't.

Agile Marketing Definition:

Customer-focused:

Agile marketing centers all decisions around the needs and wants of the client. It entails being aware of and accommodating the target audience's unique requirements and preferences. Data and input from customers are what drive the decision-making process.

Instantaneous Flexibility:

Agile marketing is distinguished by its capacity to react swiftly to shifting market dynamics. Agile marketing is flexible and adaptive to better meet the changing needs of the audience, in contrast to traditional marketing, which frequently adheres to strict plans.

Cross-functional and cooperative:

Cross-functional teamwork and collaboration are key components of agile marketing. Teams collaborate to organize, carry out, and assess marketing initiatives. Marketing tactics that are more thorough and integrated are promoted by this integrated approach.

Making Decisions Based on Data:

Agile marketing heavily relies on data and analytics. Data is essential to marketers in order to make well-informed decisions, assess the results of their work, and constantly improve their tactics.

Continual Enhancement:

Teams that use agile marketing take a "test and learn" stance. In order to create continuous changes, they test and evaluate their marketing strategies frequently, finding out what works and what doesn't. It's a culture of ongoing improvement and learning.

Openness and Responsibility:

Agile marketing promotes a transparent culture in which teams are willing to discuss their struggles, victories, and areas of growth. A core idea of accountability is that individuals and groups must accept accountability for their actions.

What Is Not Agile Marketing

Haphazard or Random Marketing:

Agile marketing does not advocate acting on the spur of the moment or carrying out marketing campaigns without a strategy. It is an organized strategy with a number of predetermined procedures and techniques.

Absence of Planning

Agile marketing does not mean that plan is lacking. Although it still necessitates a well-defined marketing plan, it permits modifications and enhancements according to current information and evolving conditions.

Exclusively Speed-Oriented:

Agile marketing emphasizes responsiveness and agility, but it goes beyond just doing things as fast as possible. It involves responding to market conditions in order to deliver value in an efficient and effective manner.

Ignore the Planning:

Agile marketing does not imply complete contempt for planning. It entails planning in shorter cycles, concentrating on the highest priority tasks, and remaining adaptable in response to input and information.

Anarchy or Absence of Structure:

Agile marketing does not equate to disarray or an absence of order. It is a methodical technique to organizing and managing marketing work that adheres to particular methodology, like Scrum or Kanban.

Only for Small Businesses:

Agile marketing is not just for startups or small companies. It may be used by businesses of all kinds, even the biggest ones, to improve their responsiveness and marketing plans.

Important Agile Marketing Principles:

Examining the fundamentals of agile marketing is necessary to comprehend the idea in its entirety. The strategy is guided by the following concepts, which distinguish it from conventional marketing strategies:

Progress that is incremental and iterative:

Marketing campaigns are divided into smaller, more doable tasks by agile marketing. These duties are completed quickly in cycles, and they are reviewed and adjusted frequently. Continuous improvement and little steps forward are made possible by this iterative process.

Customer-focusedness:

Agile marketing gives the target audience's requirements and preferences top priority. It entails talking to consumers, getting their input, and utilizing data to develop marketing tactics that appeal to the target market.

Interdepartmental Cooperation:

Agile marketing teams are made up of people with a variety of backgrounds and specialties. Teams are able to work together to accomplish shared objectives because of this integrated strategy, which promotes collaboration.

Making Decisions Based on Data:

The foundation of agile marketing is data. It helps with strategy optimization, decision-making based on facts, and gauging the success of marketing initiatives. By using a data-centric approach, marketing campaigns are guaranteed to be grounded on current knowledge.

Adaptability and Flexibility:

Agile marketing is adaptive and fluid, enabling teams to react to shifting consumer preferences and market situations. It is flexible and open to changes and advancements rather than adhering to strict plans.

Open and Honest Communication

Open and honest communication both inside the team and throughout the company is encouraged by agile marketing. Teams that routinely communicate about their accomplishments, struggles, and growth foster a collaborative and trustworthy environment.

Try and Discover:

Teams that use agile marketing adopt a "test and learn" strategy. They don't hesitate to try new things, and they utilize the findings of these endeavors to refine their tactics and make wise judgments.

Agile Approaches to Marketing:

There is no one-size-fits-all strategy for agile marketing. It requires the application of particular structures and procedures in order to successfully apply its ideas. Several well-liked agile marketing techniques consist of:

Agile:

Scrum is an agile software development methodology that groups work into time-limited iterations known as "sprints." Usually lasting between two and four weeks, each sprint produces a potentially shippable product increment. This could refer to a particular marketing campaign, piece of information, or characteristic of a product.

Kibana:

Teams can control their workflow with the use of the Kanban visual framework. To manage the status of tasks, it entails building a Kanban board and moving them through several stages, such as "To-Do," "In Progress," and "Done." Teams can manage their work more effectively and transparently with the use of this technique.

Slim:

Eliminating waste, maximizing value, and continuously improving processes are the goals of lean principles. This translates to marketing as cutting out pointless activity, concentrating on high-impact work, and routinely reviewing the workflow to make improvements.

Uses of Agile Marketing in Real-World Applications:

Agile marketing can help both B2B and B2C companies in a variety of sectors; it is not restricted to any one industry or kind of company. Here are a few real-world uses for agile marketing:

Launchpads:

Startups may effectively and economically reach their target audience with agile marketing. Startups must be able to quickly adjust their course in reaction to feedback from the market because they frequently have little funding and few resources. Without spending a fortune, agile marketing enables them to test their hypotheses, modify their plans, and increase brand recognition.

Founded Businesses:

Agile marketing may be necessary for established businesses to remain competitive in the quickly evolving market of today. These companies frequently have intricate procedures and structures, which can impede decision-making and implementation. Agile marketing can assist companies in becoming more responsive and nimble, which will allow them to introduce new goods or campaigns more rapidly and more successfully.

inventiveness

Agile marketing promotes experimentation and creativity, which in turn stimulates innovation. Teams are free to experiment with novel concepts and methods, taking lessons from both their achievements and setbacks. A brand can differentiate itself from the competition by using innovative ideas and campaigns that result from this innovative culture.

Obstacles & Things to Think About:

In order to effectively execute agile marketing, firms must tackle a number of issues and concerns:

Culture Change:

Agile marketing necessitates an organizational culture change. It demands a dedication to openness, cooperation, and ongoing education. Employees accustomed to conventional marketing strategies can object to it.

Education and Training:

The concepts and practices of agile development should be taught to marketing teams. This entails being aware of ideas like data-driven decision-making, stand-up meetings, and sprints.

Multifunctional Groups:

Create cross-functional teams by assembling people with different backgrounds and specialties. This makes it possible for marketing to take a more integrated and holistic approach, with teams cooperating to accomplish shared objectives.

Data-Driven Methodology:

Agile marketing makes judgments based on analytics and data. To assess the effectiveness of their efforts and make changes in response to real-time insights, organizations must spend money on analytics tools and collect pertinent data.

Pilot Initiatives:

It is advised to test the agile marketing approach by beginning with pilot initiatives. The process's effective adoption will be aided by lessons learned from these early encounters and process improvement.

Constant Enhancement:

Promote a culture of continuous improvement where teams evaluate their work on a regular basis and look for methods to improve its effectiveness and efficiency.

To sum up:

Agile marketing emphasizes customer-centricity, adaptability, collaboration, data-driven decision-making, iterative improvement, openness, and accountability. As a result, it marks a fundamental shift in marketing strategies and methods. It is an organized process based on distinct ideas rather than a haphazard or chaotic approach.

Companies hoping to capitalize on agile marketing's advantages and maintain their competitiveness in the ever evolving business environment must have a clear understanding of what agile marketing is and isn't. Agile marketing is flexible and can be applied in a variety of settings. It is a potent strategy that can be used by both new and established businesses to promote innovation, accelerate time to market, and increase consumer engagement. Organizations that want to succeed with agile marketing must make a culture shift commitment, make technology and training investments, and maintain ongoing process improvement. Agility is not only a competitive advantage in the fast-paced world of today; it is a need for marketers who want to prosper.

Chapter 2: Building an Agile Marketing Team.

Constructing a Flexible Marketing Group

Marketing teams need to be nimble in today's fast-paced business environment in order to remain competitive and adaptable to quickly shifting consumer behavior and market dynamics. Agile marketing is more than simply a framework; it's also about putting together and developing a team of marketers who can apply agile methods in a productive way. This essay will discuss the essential elements of assembling an agile marketing team, the competencies and attributes required of team members, and the development of an innovative and agile organizational culture.

Elements of Putting Together an Agile Marketing Team:

Multifunctional Proficiency:

A team devoted to agile marketing should include personnel with a variety of backgrounds and specialties. Experts in site development, social media management, and customer experience should be on the team in addition to traditional marketing jobs like content generation, design, SEO, and data analysis. Cross-functional teams make sure that every facet of marketing is addressed and that the group is capable of handling a variety of tasks without the need for outside personnel.

Specialization in Roles:

The cross-functional team should have members with specialized roles. Each team member should have a primary job or responsibility within the group, even though they may each have a broad skill set. By assigning particular duties to people who are most qualified to execute them, this specialization guarantees efficiency and effectiveness.

Unambiguous Communication

Agile marketing places a strong emphasis on teamwork and communication. Each member of the team needs to be able to communicate ideas, share developments, and give constructive criticism. For the team to work well together, there must be open lines of communication, frequent team meetings, and collaborative tools.

Tools and Technology:

A marketing team that is agile must have access to the appropriate tools and technology. This comprises communication platforms, analytics tools, and project management software that promote teamwork and expedite productivity. Appropriate tools can improve the efficiency and production of a team.

Direction and Leadership:

To establish priorities, assign responsibilities, and guarantee that the team remains in line with the organization's objectives, every team need competent leadership. Leadership should support creativity and offer direction without restricting team autonomy.

Ongoing Education and Training:

Team members should make a commitment to lifelong learning because the field of digital marketing is constantly changing. It is essential to have access to resources and training programs in order to stay current with developing technology and industry trends.

Member attributes and competencies of an agile marketing team:

Flexibility:

Members of an agile marketing team need to be flexible and ready to adjust to changing market conditions. When the need comes, they ought to be prepared to quickly change course and adopt fresh tactics.

Data-Based:

An essential competency for members of an agile marketing team is the capacity for data-driven decision-making. They ought to be adept at analyzing data and capable of drawing conclusions from a range of analytics instruments.

Creativity & Innovation:

Agile marketing requires creative thinking. It is important to support team members in thinking creatively, coming up with fresh concepts, and trying out novel strategies.

Successful Interaction:

Effective communication is essential to agile marketing, both inside the team and with external stakeholders. Members of the team should be able to actively listen to criticism and communicate ideas clearly.

Time Handling:

Agile marketing frequently calls for juggling several projects at once. To guarantee that assignments are finished on time and that team members can efficiently divide their responsibility, good time management is essential.

Solving Issues:

Agile marketing teams face a variety of difficulties that call for original problem-solving techniques. Members of a team should be adept at recognizing problems, coming up with fixes, and acting to get things done.

Building a Culture of Agile Marketing:

Creating an environment that encourages flexibility, creativity, and teamwork is just as important as having the correct mix of abilities when putting together an agile marketing team. This is how you do it:

Autonomy and Empowerment:

Give team members the freedom to decide for themselves and try out novel strategies to empower them. Motivate them to be responsible for their job and have faith in their abilities.

Cooperation and Openness:

Encourage an environment that values openness and cooperation. Collaboration requires regular team meetings, open lines of communication, and a readiness to discuss obstacles and successes.

Fast Fail, Quick Learn:

Promote the "fail fast, learn fast" philosophy. Innovation will inevitably involve mistakes. It should be easy for team members to take chances and learn from both achievements and setbacks.

Constant Enhancement:

Encourage a culture of continuous improvement by routinely evaluating team procedures, getting input from team members, and pinpointing areas that could use better.

Education and Training:

Make an investment in your team members' education and growth. To assist team members in staying current and developing their skill set, give them access to resources, training courses, and growth opportunities.

Honor accomplishments:

Honor both group and individual accomplishments. Team morale and motivation are increased by praise and constructive criticism.

Receptive to Input:

Urge members of the team to actively seek out and be receptive to feedback from other team members as well as external stakeholders. Giving constructive criticism is an effective way to make improvements.

Customer-focusedness:

Instill in the team a customer-centric mindset. Instruct team members to comprehend the requirements, inclinations, and actions of customers and use this understanding to marketing tactics.

Agile Approaches:

Use agile techniques to direct the team's work on tasks and projects, such as Scrum, Kanban, or Lean. Agile techniques are given a defined foundation by these methodologies.

Developing an Agile Marketing Team Presents Difficulties:

Although assembling an agile marketing team has many benefits, there are drawbacks that businesses must consider:

Culture Change:

There may be opposition to switching from an agile marketing strategy to a traditional one. It could be difficult at first for team members used to established procedures to adjust to new working methods.

Restrictions on Resources:

It could be necessary to invest in additional resources like software, technology, and training in order to build an agile marketing team. To meet the demands of the team, organizations must carefully distribute their resources.

Management and Leadership:

A team that practices agile marketing has to be guided by effective leaders. The performance of the team may be hampered by inexperienced or unprepared leadership.

Control and Autonomy in Balance:

It might be difficult to strike a balance between the requirement for supervision and control and team liberty. Companies need to strike the correct balance between allowing teams to innovate and upholding company standards and goals.

Examples of Cases

Let's examine a few case studies to see how businesses have effectively created agile marketing teams:

HubPage:

Agile marketing ideas have been adopted by HubSpot, a prominent provider of inbound marketing and sales tools. The business put together cross-functional teams of developers, designers, and marketers. These teams have greatly enhanced their capacity to react to changes in the market and consumer input by working in sprints and utilizing Scrum methodology.

Soundcloud:

The massive music streaming company Spotify improved its marketing efforts by implementing agile marketing techniques. They manage marketing campaigns, swiftly iterate on tactics, and adjust to real-time customer input by utilizing agile approaches. With this strategy, Spotify has been able to maintain its competitiveness in the ever-evolving music streaming market.

Creating an agile marketing team is crucial for businesses hoping to prosper in the quick-changing and hectic commercial world. It entails putting together a cross-functional team with a range of expertise, encouraging an innovative and adaptable culture, and helping team members acquire the required abilities and traits.

In order to achieve success, firms must foster a culture of continuous improvement, empower team members, promote collaboration and transparency, and offer chances for training and growth. Building an agile marketing team might be difficult, but the rewards of better customer interaction, more responsiveness, and enhanced marketing tactics make it an investment worth making for businesses looking to stay competitive in the fast-paced marketing environment of today.

The Key Roles in an Agile Marketing Team.

Crucial Positions in an Agile Marketing Group

Agile marketing is a cutting-edge, extremely flexible method of marketing that helps teams react quickly to shifts in the market and client demands. The correct balance of roles within the team is crucial for implementing agile marketing successfully. The main tasks of an agile marketing team, as well as how they work together to create effective marketing campaigns, will all be covered in this essay.

1. Owner of Product:

In an agile marketing team, the Product Owner plays a key role in establishing the objectives, priorities, and vision of marketing initiatives. The marketing team and other stakeholders, including sales teams and executives, are liaised between by this job. The duties of a product owner consist of:

deciding on the marketing efforts' strategic direction.
arranging marketing campaigns according to importance and fit with the objectives of the company.
establishing the goals and requirements of the project.
acting as the "voice of the customer" to make sure that demands are met by marketing initiatives.
2. Scrum Lead:

The Scrum Master is in charge of guiding the team through agile marketing processes, making sure they adhere to agile standards, and removing roadblocks to advancement. This position promotes agile ideas and practices while acting as a coach and mentor for the marketing team. The duties of the Scrum Master comprise:

managing the daily stand-up meetings, sprint evaluations, and sprint planning.
directing the group to follow the concepts and practices of agile.
encouraging team members to communicate and work together.
locating and removing obstacles that could stand in the way of the team's advancement.

3. Manager of Marketing:

Overseeing the daily marketing operations and making sure the team's efforts are in line with the organization's marketing strategy are important responsibilities of the marketing manager. In this function, a variety of marketing initiatives and activities are coordinated and managed. The duties of the marketing manager consist of:

creating and carrying out marketing strategy and plans.
Tracking advertising performance and evaluating campaign efficacy.
working together to establish goals and KPIs (key performance indicators).
Organizing resources and spending for marketing.
4. Expert in Content:

When it comes to producing and overseeing material that appeals to the intended audience, content specialists are essential. They are in charge of creating interesting and captivating material for blogs, social media, email marketing, and other platforms. The duties of content specialists consist of:

creating and preserving a calendar of material.
producing excellent written and visual content that complements the marketing plan.
content optimization for both user experience and search engines (SEO).
interacting with the public on social media and through the information they consume.

5. Artist for Graphics:

In order to provide aesthetically appealing assets, such pictures, infographics, and videos, that complement marketing campaigns and materials, graphic designers are crucial. They make certain that the design components properly engage the audience and are consistent with the brand's visual identity. Responsibilities of graphic designers include:

creating marketing materials, including social media graphics, banners, and brochures.
producing aesthetically appealing material for adverts and websites.
working together as a team to develop and implement design concepts.
ensuring that all visual elements adhere to the same brand.

6. Analyst of Data:

Data analysts are essential to agile marketing because they offer data-driven insights that help inform choices and maximize marketing initiatives. To assess the effectiveness of marketing initiatives and strategies, they are in charge of gathering, examining, and interpreting data. The duties of data analysts include:

collecting and analyzing information from a range of sources, including as social media metrics, website analytics, and consumer behavior.
delivering suggestions based on data to enhance marketing performance.
generating dashboards and reports to monitor KPIs and calculate ROI.
utilizing data analysis to find possibilities and trends.

7. Expert in SEO:

Specialists in search engine optimization (SEO) concentrate on improving online content to raise a website's organic traffic and search engine rankings. They are essential in making sure that the intended audience can find marketing initiatives. Among the duties of SEO specialists are:

finding pertinent search terms by performing keyword research.
enhancing the meta descriptions, tags, and content of websites for search engines.

tracking and reporting website traffic and search engine rankings.
keeping up with algorithm modifications and SEO best practices.

8. Web Master:

The organization's website is made and maintained by web developers, who also make sure it is responsive, functional, and easy to use. They are essential in helping marketing campaigns and efforts with their technological components. The duties of web developers include:

constructing and maintaining the website in accordance with marketing objectives and plans.

ensuring the functionality and responsiveness of websites on different devices.

working together as a team to create improvements and modifications to the website.
resolving website-related technical problems.

9. Manager of Social Media:

Social media managers concentrate on creating and implementing social media strategies to interact with the public, promote brands, and enhance website traffic. They are essential to keeping an interesting and active internet presence. The duties of social media managers consist of:

content creation and curation for social media networks.

Taking care of social media profiles and planning content.

interacting with the viewer by sending out messages, comments, and dialogues.

tracking social media analytics to evaluate results and modify tactics.

10. Expert in Email Marketing:

The task of organizing and carrying out email marketing campaigns falls to email marketing specialists. Through email communication, they are essential for lead nurturing, client retention, and conversion optimization. The duties of email marketing specialists consist of:

creating and preserving a calendar for email marketing.

Email lists are created and segmented to enable targeted communication.

creating engaging email content, such as promotions, newsletters, and customized communications.

email campaign performance measurement and strategy optimization through the use of metrics.

11. Expert in Paid Promotion:

The creation and management of paid advertising campaigns across a variety of platforms, including social media and Google Ads, is the primary responsibility of paid advertising specialists. They oversee the distribution of funds, maximizing return on investment, and enhancing ad performance. The duties of Paid Advertising Specialists consist of:

creating and putting into practice sponsored advertising plans.

developing and refining advertising programs to meet marketing objectives.

coordinating bidding tactics and advertising expenditures.

Metrics related to advertising are tracked and analyzed to determine their efficacy.

12. Specialist in Customer Experience (CX):

CX specialists are in charge of making sure that every encounter with the brand and the client is favorable, dependable, and consistent with the company's principles. They are essential in raising client loyalty and satisfaction. Tasks performed by CX Specialists include:

mapping and examining the pathways and touchpoints with customers. determining areas where the customer experience has to be improved and where problems exist.

working together as a team to execute improvements and adjustments to improve CX.

keeping an eye on customer satisfaction data and feedback.
Working Together and Communicating:

Success in an agile marketing team depends on people working well together and communicating with one another. Each function collaborates with others to develop and carry out marketing strategies, and it also adds to the team's overall objectives. The roles work together as follows:

Scrum Structure:

The Scrum framework is frequently used by agile marketing teams, and the Scrum Master facilitates team meetings and makes sure the team adheres to agile principles. While team members collaborate to design and carry out marketing campaigns in brief cycles known as sprints, the Product Owner establishes priorities and targets.

Interdepartmental Cooperation:

The team's many roles work together to handle every facet of marketing. Data analysts track performance, SEO specialists optimize for search engines, graphic designers supply images, and content specialists develop content. The implementation of a cross-functional strategy guarantees the comprehensiveness and depth of marketing initiatives.

Making Decisions Based on Data:

Data analysts offer insights derived from data analysis to support strategy optimization and decision-making. Based on performance data, the team uses these insights to make real-time adjustments to marketing campaigns.

Constant Enhancement:

Teams that use agile marketing promote a continuous improvement culture. During retrospectives, which are facilitated by the scrum master, team members evaluate their work, pinpoint areas for development, and make adjustments to improve their procedures.

Developing Agile Marketing Teams Presents Difficulties:

There are obstacles to overcome while creating an agile marketing team, and these are what businesses must do to succeed:

Culture Change:

There may be opposition to switching from traditional to agile marketing. It could be difficult at first for team members used to established procedures to adjust to new working methods.

Restrictions on Resources:

It could be necessary to invest in additional resources like software, technology, and training in order to build an agile marketing team. To meet the demands of the team, organizations must carefully distribute their resources.

Management and Leadership:

A team that practices agile marketing has to be guided by effective leaders. The performance of the team may be hampered by inexperienced or unprepared leadership.

Control and Autonomy in Balance:

It might be difficult to strike a balance between the requirement for supervision and control and team liberty. Companies need to strike the correct balance between allowing teams to innovate and upholding company standards and goals.

Example Study:

To further understand how an agile marketing team may work together, let's examine a fictional case study:

XYZ Tech Solutions, the company

Team Organization:

Scrum Master: Mark, Marketing Manager: Sarah, Content Specialist: Mike, Graphic Designer: Lisa, Data Analyst: Emily, Product Owner: Jane Expert in SEO: Alex

Chris, a web developer

Customer Experience (CX) Specialist: Daniel; Paid Advertising Specialist: Amanda; Social Media Manager: Olivia; Email Marketing Specialist: Jason Cooperation and Flow of Work:

First Week of Sprint Planning: The team gets together to arrange the next sprint. The sprint's priorities and objectives are determined by Jane, the product owner. The group talks about possible campaign concepts, and each role states what their particular duties and obligations are.

Execution of the Sprint (Third to Third Weeks): During the sprint, each team member works on their assigned tasks. Emails are designed, adverts are published, content is written, and designs are made. The website is updated when necessary, thanks to the efforts of Chris, the web developer.

Every day, the team members convene for a quick stand-up meeting to review the day's progress, exchange any difficulties, and give updates. The Scrum Master, Mark, makes sure that obstacles are dealt with as soon as possible.

Fourth Week Sprint Review: To evaluate the results of their work, the team does a sprint review. After Emily, the data analyst, shares her observations on the campaign's performance, the team talks about what went well and what needs improvement.

Fourth Week Retrospective: To evaluate the sprint's accomplishments and opportunities for development, the team convenes a retrospective. They talk about how to improve teamwork and output in the upcoming sprint.

Result:

The XYZ Tech Solutions agile marketing team works well together to plan and carry out marketing strategies. The team's ability to collaborate in brief cycles allows it to modify strategy instantly in response to customer input and performance indicators. They are able to remain productive and responsive in the quick-paced tech sector because to this iterative methodology.

Organizations hoping to prosper in the dynamic and constantly shifting marketing landscape must build an agile marketing team with the proper balance of jobs and cultivate a collaborative culture. Each team member brings special talents and knowledge to the table to help develop and carry out successful marketing initiatives. The success of an agile marketing team is largely dependent on efficient cooperation, transparent communication, and a dedication to data-driven decision-making. Organizations can use agile marketing to be competitive and responsive to changes in the market and client needs by tackling obstacles and streamlining their workflows.

Cultivating a Culture of Collaboration and Innovation

Developing an Innovative and Collaborative Culture

Organizations need to continuously innovate and adapt in today's ever changing business environment in order to be relevant and competitive. To encourage innovation, creativity, and problem-solving, an innovative and collaborative culture is necessary for growth. This essay will discuss the value of developing such a culture, the essential components that make it up, and the doable actions that businesses can do to foster an atmosphere that promotes creativity and teamwork.

The Importance of Innovation and Teamwork:

Innovation and teamwork are not just catchphrases; they are essential elements of a robust and successful company. This is why they are important:

A competitive edge

Organizations that can innovate quickly and work well together will be in a better position to stand out from the competition and adapt to changing client wants in a market that is becoming more global and competitive.

Flexibility:

Organizations can adjust to shifting market conditions, technological advancements, and consumer preferences through cooperation and innovation. In industries that are constantly changing, they are indispensable.

Issue-Solving:

It is simpler to take on difficult problems and come up with innovative solutions in collaborative settings since they bring together a variety of viewpoints and levels of experience.

Staff Involvement

Employee engagement and happiness can be increased by an environment that values creativity and teamwork. Employees are more motivated and dedicated when they are given the opportunity to share their thoughts and understand the results of their labor.

Customer-focusedness:

Businesses that innovate and work together frequently get a better grasp of the wants and needs of their clients. A more customer-focused strategy may result in improved goods and services.

Important Components of an Innovative and Collaborative Culture:

Establishing a collaborative and innovative culture requires several key components:

Transparent Communication

Collaboration and innovation require an open and transparent communication infrastructure. It should facilitate unrestricted communication between team members and between departments in terms of ideas, criticism, and information. An atmosphere that fosters creativity is produced when staff members are at ease sharing their ideas.

Inclusion and Diversity:

Diverse viewpoints, experiences, and backgrounds are brought together in a diverse and inclusive workplace. This diversity can lead to a wide range of ideas and approaches, boosting innovative thinking and problem-solving.

Encouragement:

Employees that feel empowered are more inclined to take the initiative, make fresh suggestions, and work well together. Employers should encourage and mentor their staff members while granting them the liberty to experiment and make decisions on their own.

Ongoing Education:

Maintaining an ongoing learning process is essential for an innovative culture. Employers should make training and development investments in order to keep staff members abreast of emerging trends, technology, and best practices.

Failure-Rapid Attitude:

Promoting a "fail-fast" mindset entails accepting that mistakes are a necessary component of the creative process. Employees in businesses who see failure as a teaching opportunity rather than a setback are more inclined to attempt new things and take chances.

Appreciation and Incentives:

It is essential to acknowledge and thank staff members for their contributions to creativity and teamwork. This could take the kind of pay raises, incentives, or just plain acknowledgment of their hard work. Rewards aid in retaining and inspiring elite talent.

Multifunctional Groups:

To work on particular projects, cross-functional teams bring together people from various departments and backgrounds. These groups encourage the exchange of different viewpoints and specialties, which produces creative solutions.

Resource Distribution:

It is imperative for organizations to distribute resources, such as finance and time, to facilitate collaboration and creativity. This indicates a dedication to supporting a creative culture.

Encouraging Leadership:

A leader's influence over an organization's culture is significant. Establishing a culture of cooperation and innovation via visionary and supportive leadership sets the standard for the entire workforce.

How to Foster Innovation and Collaboration in Real World Settings:

The following concrete actions can be taken by organizations to foster a culture of innovation and cooperation:

Establish Specific Goals:

Establish precise, well-defined goals for cooperation and innovation. Make sure these goals are in line with the organization's overarching mission and vision.

Leadership Dedication:

Leaders ought to set a good example and show that they are dedicated to cooperation and creativity. Motivate them to contribute their own ideas and actively participate in group projects.

Form Teams with Cross-Functions:

Create cross-functional teams to address opportunities or challenging situations. These groups can foster creativity by bringing together a range of expertise and viewpoints.

Open Source Idea Exchanges:

Provide venues or avenues for staff members to contribute their ideas, such as suggestion boxes, online forums, or frequent brainstorming meetings.

Seminars on Innovation:

Plan training sessions or seminars on innovation to provide staff members the skills and knowledge they need to come up with original ideas and find novel solutions to challenges.

Reward Cycles:

Put feedback tools in place to get opinions from staff members across the board. Respond to criticism and show them that you appreciate their suggestions.

Initiatives for Inclusion and Diversity:

Encourage inclusiveness and diversity in the workplace to attract a range of viewpoints and concepts. Encourage each employee to feel accepted and a part of the team.

Programs for Acknowledgment and Reward:

Create programs for incentives and recognition that recognize and honor creative contributions. These initiatives have the power to inspire staff members to actively participate in creative and cooperative endeavors.

Testing and Prototyping:

Prior to a large-scale implementation, promote the creation of prototypes and the testing of novel concepts. Iterative improvements are possible and risk is minimized with this method.

Chapter 3: Agile Marketing Frameworks and Methodologies.

Methodologies and Frameworks for Agile Marketing

Traditional marketing strategies are frequently too inflexible and sluggish to keep up with the needs of the market and customers in today's fast-paced and always changing business environment. Because of this, a lot of marketing teams are using agile approaches to increase their efficacy, reactivity, and flexibility. We will explore many frameworks and approaches that have arisen to enable marketing teams to flourish in dynamic situations as we dig into the world of agile marketing in this essay.

Gaining insight via Agile Marketing:

Agile marketing is a collaborative, iterative approach to marketing that prioritizes data-driven decision-making, adaptability, customer-centricity, and ongoing development. The Agile Manifesto, which was first developed for software development, is where the fundamental ideas of agile marketing originate. They have been modified to fit the needs of the marketing industry.

Values of the Agile Manifesto:

People and their interactions rather than procedures and equipment.
Practical fixes as opposed to extensive documentation.
Client cooperation as opposed to contract drafting.
Adapting to change as opposed to sticking to a plan.
These ideas are embraced by agile marketing, which motivates marketing teams to:

Give customers' wants and comments first priority.
Accept adaptation and flexibility.

Work cross-functionally and cooperatively.

Measure and improve your marketing activities on a constant basis.

Agile marketing offers a variety of frameworks and processes that marketing teams can use in accordance with their unique requirements and goals, rather than taking a one-size-fits-all strategy. Let's examine some of the most well-known frameworks and approaches for agile marketing.

Scrum 1.

One of the most popular agile frameworks for software development is called Scrum. It has, nevertheless, also found application in agile marketing. The Scrum methodology places a strong emphasis on working in brief bursts, or sprints, that last two to four weeks. This is the adaptation of Scrum for marketing:

Key responsibilities defined by Scrum include the Product Owner, who assigns marketing tasks based on priority, and the Scrum Master, who makes sure the team adheres to agile methods.

Sprints: To produce noticeable results quickly, marketing teams organize and carry out marketing duties in short bursts.

Daily Stand-Ups: The group gets together every day to talk about goals, obstacles, and advancements.

Sprint Review: The team evaluates the outcomes and gets input at the conclusion of every sprint.

Retrospective: To evaluate the sprint and pinpoint areas for improvement, the team has a retrospective.

Marketing teams working on campaigns, new product launches, or other projects with well-defined goals and deadlines might benefit from Scrum. It guarantees congruence with organizational goals and encourages a methodical approach.

2. Kanji

Another agile paradigm for marketing that places an emphasis on controlling flow, restricting work-in-progress, and visualizing work is called Kanban. Kanban boards are frequently used in the marketing domain to depict marketing tasks at various levels of completion, enabling teams to monitor advancement and streamline processes.

Key elements of marketing-related Kanban:

Visual Boards: Kanban boards are used to display marketing tasks along with their respective statuses.

Work in Progress (WIP) Limits: To avoid overburdening team members and preserve a constant flow of work, teams establish WIP limits.

Continuous Flow: As a task advances from conception to completion, it passes through the Kanban board.

Pull System: When they have time, team members select tasks from the "To Do" column.

Marketing teams that handle repetitive and continuous tasks like customer service, social media management, and content production will find Kanban very helpful.

3. Marketing Lean:

Lean marketing emphasizes removing waste, providing value to clients, and streamlining procedures. It was influenced by lean manufacturing concepts. Lean marketing's fundamental ideas are frequently summed up as follows:

Customer Value: Determining what matters to customers and effectively providing it.

Continuous Improvement: Constantly looking for ways to get more effective and efficient.

Cutting Waste: Getting rid of any procedures, undertakings, or assets that don't immediately support the delivery of value.

Flow: Making certain that the task proceeds without hiccups.
Marketing teams are encouraged by lean marketing to examine their procedures, get rid of waste, and provide value to clients with as little waste as possible.

4. Manifesto for Agile Marketing:

The Agile Marketing Manifesto offers a set of guiding principles for agile marketing teams, much as the Agile Manifesto for software development. It highlights ideals and concepts like:

Validated Learning Over Opinions and Conventions: Making marketing decisions based on factual information and genuine input.

Collaboration Focused on the Customer Above Silos and Hierarchy: Fostering departmental and team collaboration to develop a customer-centric marketing strategy.

Smaller, more flexible efforts that can adjust to market shifts are preferred than larger, more ambitious ones.

Choosing to embrace a process of trial and discovery over static prediction might help you better understand the requirements and preferences of your customers.

Marketing teams can use the Agile Marketing Manifesto as a framework to embrace agile concepts and develop a more flexible and customer-focused marketing strategy.

5. AMM, or Agile Marketing Methodology:

The Agile Marketing Methodology is a comprehensive approach that integrates agile concepts with a structured process. It was developed by the Agile Marketing Academy. It provides a methodical approach to integrating agile marketing within a company. Important elements of the AMM consist of:

Establishing Goals: Clearly outlining the goals and key results (OKRs) of marketing initiatives.

Cross-functional Scrum teams are formed to carry out marketing duties.
Backlog prioritization is the process of ranking marketing work in a backlog according to importance to customers.

Planning marketing efforts in two-week sprints with clear objectives and assignments is known as sprint planning.

Daily Stand-Ups: To keep the team in sync, have daily stand-up meetings.
Sprint Review: Analyzing each sprint's outcomes and getting input.
Retrospective: Examining the sprint and pinpointing areas in need of development.

For businesses seeking a methodical strategy to embracing agility, the Agile Marketing Methodology presents a defined approach to agile marketing implementation that makes it a viable option.

6. Marketing for Growth:

A specific kind of agile marketing, growth marketing emphasizes ongoing experimentation and data-driven decision-making. The concepts of growth hacking are central to it, with a focus on quick testing, measurement, and optimization. Crucial components of development marketing consist of:

A/B testing: Examining various marketing strategies to see which ones produce the greatest outcomes.

Iterative experimentation is the process of continuously testing out novel concepts and tactics in order to spur expansion.

Making marketing decisions based on analytics and data rather than conjecture is known as "data-driven decision-making."

Using a user-centric approach means centering marketing initiatives around the demands and behaviors of the consumer and developing tactics accordingly.

For businesses looking to expand quickly and measurablely and prepared to make the investment in a culture of experimentation and adaptability, growth marketing is perfect.

7. Focused on the customer:

The customer is the focal point of all marketing initiatives in customer-centric marketing. Deep comprehension of consumer demands, interests, and behaviors is emphasized. Among the fundamental tenets of customer-centric marketing are:

Persona Development: Developing comprehensive profiles of customers in order to more effectively target and customize marketing campaigns.

Customer journey mapping is the process of comprehending the complete customer journey in order to provide engaging and customized experiences. Feedback loops: Constantly collecting and evaluating consumer input to enhance marketing tactics.

Personalization: Tailoring content and marketing messaging to each individual customer.

In today's competitive marketplace, when customer experience and personalization are critical differentiators, customer-centric marketing is imperative.

8. Sleek Startup Promotion:

Lean Startup Marketing, which is based on the Lean Startup process, is concentrated on rapidly and effectively evaluating concepts in order to prevent squandering resources on unsuccessful marketing efforts. Lean Startup Marketing's essential components include:

Minimum Viable Marketing (MVM): Putting into practice the tiniest, most crucial marketing initiatives in order to collect information and test hypotheses.

Build-Measure-Learn (BML) is the process of creating a marketing campaign, assessing its effectiveness, and drawing conclusions from the data. Decide whether to change course or stick with the marketing strategy in light of the information acquired.

Iterative marketing is the process of fine-tuning marketing strategy by repeatedly going through the BML cycle.

For startups and small firms trying to maximize their marketing efforts with constrained resources, lean startup marketing is a useful strategy.

Obstacles to Agile Marketing Adoption:

Even while agile marketing has many advantages, some businesses may find it difficult to implement. Typical difficulties include:

Cultural Shift: Making the transition from traditional to agile marketing frequently necessitates a big cultural shift inside the company. One potential obstacle is resistance to change.

Allocation of Resources: Investing in technology, tools, and training may be necessary for agile marketing. To facilitate the shift, organizations must strategically deploy their resources.

Leadership Buy-In: For agile concepts to be successfully adopted, leadership support and dedication are necessary.

Finding the Optimal Balance between Team Autonomy and the Requirement for Supervision and Control: This can be a Difficult Affair.

IBM's Agile Marketing Transformation Case Study:

The multinational consulting and technology giant IBM made a big change to embrace agile marketing. The business gave its marketing teams access to a range of agile frameworks, including Scrum and Kanban. The following were the main actions in IBM's agile marketing transformation:

IBM's leadership demonstrated a strong commitment to the transition, acknowledging the need for flexibility.

Agile Training: In order to provide marketing teams with the skills and knowledge they need, the company made an investment in agile training and workshops.

IBM created cross-functional teams in order to promote communication and cooperation among team members.

Iterative Campaigns: In order to swiftly obtain data and feedback, marketing teams began concentrating on tiny, iterative campaigns.

IBM incorporated agile project management tools and technologies to enhance workflow management and promote teamwork.

Improved campaign success and customer engagement resulted from the change, which enabled IBM's marketing teams to become more responsive and customer-centric.

Marketing teams can achieve their objectives in a more flexible and customer-focused manner by utilizing agile marketing frameworks and processes. Organizations can select the agile framework that best suits their needs and goals, from Scrum and Kanban to Lean Startup Marketing and customer-centric tactics.

Adoption success depends on leadership support, a willingness to accept agile principles, and a commitment to cultural change. Marketing teams may succeed in fast-paced, cutthroat situations by putting the needs of their customers first, encouraging teamwork, and making data-driven decisions. Agile marketing will continue to be a crucial tool for being adaptable, successful, and creative as the corporate environment changes.

Scrum, Kanban, Lean, and Other Agile Frameworks

An Detailed Overview of Scrum, Kanban, Lean, and Other Agile Frameworks

Agile frameworks are being adopted by organizations from a variety of industries to improve their development processes, project management, and general efficiency in the fast-paced and constantly-evolving corporate world of today. Agile approaches facilitate cooperation, adaptation, and continuous improvement by providing a flexible and customer-centric approach. Scrum, Kanban, and Lean are some of the most well-known and often applied agile frameworks. These three fundamental frameworks, together with other agile approaches, their applications, guiding principles, and the ways in which adopting them benefits organizations will all be covered in this essay.

Agile:

One of the most well-known and well-established agile frameworks is scrum. Originally created for software development, it is currently used in project management, product development, marketing, and other areas. It is based on the core ideas of flexibility, incremental progress, and teamwork.

Crucial Elements of Scrum:

Roles: Scrum outlines distinct roles for the Development Team, Scrum Master, and Product Owner. The Development Team completes the tasks, the Scrum Master makes sure agile principles are followed, and the Product Owner sets the priorities for the work.

Sprints: Scrum work is divided into time-boxed units called sprints, which are typically two to four weeks in length. Delivering a potentially shippable product increment is the goal of each sprint.

Product Backlog: The tasks or user stories that need to be finished are listed in order of priority in the product backlog. This list is managed and updated on a regular basis by the product owner.

Daily Stand-Ups: Teams convene for daily stand-ups, sometimes known as "daily scrums," to talk about objectives, difficulties, and advancements.

Sprint Review: To showcase finished work and get input, the team has a sprint review at the conclusion of each sprint.

Retrospective: To discuss what went well and what could be improved, a retrospective is done following each sprint review.

Scrum applications:

Scrum is adaptable and useful in many different fields and contexts, such as project management, product development, marketing campaigns, and software development. It works well for projects with clear goals and deadlines because of its emphasis on organized work sprints and iterative development.

Advantages of Scrum

enhanced cross-functional team collaboration and communication.
improved flexibility in response to modifications and client input.
improved accountability and openness with clearly defined roles and responsibilities.
quicker value delivery through iterative development.
improved risk control and increased client contentment.
Kibana:

Another agile approach, Kanban, emphasizes flow management, work in progress (WIP) limitation, and work visualization. Kanban, which has its roots in the Toyota Production System, is becoming more and more well-known in the fields of operations, software development, and project management.

Crucial Elements of Kanban:

Visual Boards: Teams can see the work flow and spot bottlenecks by using Kanban's visual boards, which show work items and their status.

Work in Progress (WIP) Limits: To avoid overburdening team members and maintain a continuous flow, teams set WIP limits for each stage of the project.

Continuous Flow: As work items advance from the point of initiation to the point of completion, they are dragged through the Kanban board, and new items are added only when space permits.

Pull System: As team members are able to handle them, work items are pulled from one column to the next in a Kanban system.

Kanban applications:

Teams working on continuous, repeated projects and procedures, such content production, customer service, and software maintenance, benefit greatly from the use of Kanban. It provides a useful and graphical method for monitoring tasks, streamlining workflows, and guaranteeing timely completion of work.

Advantages of Kanban:

enhanced clarity on tasks and obstructions.

increased adaptability to handle various job kinds.
enhanced flow and lessening of the team's workload.
improved work management transparency and efficiency.
flexibility in responding to shifting priorities and developments.
Slim:

Lean is an agile framework that prioritizes value delivery, waste removal, and process optimization. It was influenced by the ideas of the Toyota Production System. Project management, services, manufacturing, and other operations can all benefit from the application of lean principles.

Crucial Elements of Lean:

Value Stream Mapping: Value stream mapping is the first step in lean methodology. It helps to visualize and identify inefficiencies and waste throughout the entire process.

Waste Elimination: Lean identifies and gets rid of eight different kinds of waste, such as waiting, overproduction, flaws, and needless movement.

Continuous Improvement: Lean encourages teams to continuously look for methods to streamline operations and provide value in a more effective manner.

Pull Systems: Lean use pull systems, much like Kanban, to make sure that work is started based on consumer demand rather than overproduction.

Implementing Lean:

Many industries, including manufacturing, healthcare, supply chain management, and project management, can benefit from lean implementations. Numerous corporate objectives are aligned with its focus on delivering value, streamlining processes, and removing waste.

Advantages of Lean:

decreased waste and financial savings.
cycle durations and process efficiency are increased.
improved client happiness and quality.

a continual improvement culture.
Better alignment of work with consumer demand.

Other Frameworks for Agile:

Apart from Scrum, Kanban, and Lean, various more agile frameworks and approaches have surfaced to address certain requirements and sectors. Let's examine a few of these frameworks and how they are used:

XP stands for extreme programming.

A software development style called Extreme Programming (XP) places a strong emphasis on close communication between engineers and clients. In order to guarantee high-quality software and client happiness, it encourages techniques like pair programming, continuous integration, and test-driven development.

Applications: XP is perfect for projects involving the development of high-caliber, quickly changing software with a strong emphasis on client needs.

2. Agile Delivery with Discipline (DAD):

A process decision framework called Disciplined Agile Delivery (DAD) combines a number of lean and agile methodologies to offer a holistic solution for complicated projects. DAD is flexible enough to accommodate various project kinds thanks to its array of lifecycle choices.

Applications: DAD works well for large-scale projects that call for adaptability and a blend of different agile methodologies.

3. The SAFe, or Scaled Agile Framework:

For major firms wishing to deploy agile at scale, the Scaled Agile Framework (SAFe) was created. SAFe offers an organized method for implementing agile concepts across several teams and divisions.

Applications: SAFe is perfect for big businesses looking to guarantee agile principles, alignment, and cooperation throughout a complicated enterprise.

4. FDD, or feature-driven development:

The goal of the feature-driven development (FDD) process is to construct software by segmenting it into discrete, well-defined features. Iterative development and incremental delivery are used to create each feature.

Applications: Software development initiatives that aim to offer precise, well-defined features in an organized way can benefit from FDD.

5. The DSDM, or Dynamic Systems Development Method:

Rapid software delivery is the goal of the agile framework known as the Dynamic Systems Development Method (DSDM). It places a strong emphasis on client participation, teamwork, and a development process that is time-boxed.

Applications: Software development projects where quick delivery and client involvement are top priorities can benefit from the use of DSDM.

Case Study: Spotify's Agile Transformation

The metamorphosis of Spotify is a noteworthy example of agile adoption gone right. The massive music streaming company developed "The Spotify Model," an agile methodology based on Scrum and Kanban. Important aspects of their agile methodology include of:

"Squads" are cross-functional groups that operate independently on particular characteristics.

Squads are arranged into bigger units known as "tribes" that have common goals.
a mindset that values team members' individuality, experimentation, and ongoing learning.

Spotify is a paradigm for agile adoption in the digital sector thanks to its agile transformation, which allowed them to develop quickly, offer new products, and react to user feedback.

Organizations can approach project management and process optimization in a dynamic and customer-focused manner by utilizing agile frameworks and techniques such as Scrum, Kanban, Lean, and others. These frameworks can be customized to fit different sectors and project types, even if they have similar characteristics like flexibility, cooperation, and continual improvement.

The particular objectives and needs of the organization determine which agile framework is best. Agile approaches offer a path to success in today's quickly evolving corporate environment, whether it is through improving software development, streamlining processes, or completing customer-centric projects. Through the implementation of agile frameworks and concepts, firms may adapt to changing circumstances, meet customer demands, and continuously enhance their operations.

Applying Agile Principles to Marketing.

Using Agile Concepts in Marketing: A Success Road Map

Because of the quick changes in customer behavior, technology, and competition, the marketing environment is always changing. Many marketing teams are using agile techniques and principles, which were first created for software development, to overcome these obstacles and maintain their competitiveness. Agile marketing is an attitude and methodology that helps marketing teams to be flexible, give priority to the needs of their customers, and keep refining their tactics. This essay will look at the advantages of using agile concepts in marketing, how marketing teams may adopt these ideas, and how marketing can benefit from them.

Comprehending Agile Marketing Principles:

The Agile Manifesto, a collection of ideals and guidelines developed by software engineers to encourage adaptability, teamwork, and customer-centricity, is the foundation of agile concepts. The Agile Manifesto's fundamental principles are:

People and their interactions rather than procedures and equipment.
Practical fixes as opposed to extensive documentation.
Client cooperation as opposed to contract drafting.

Adapting to change as opposed to sticking to a plan.

These principles place a strong emphasis on the value of people, flexibility, input from customers, and incremental development. These ideas, when used in marketing, produce an agile marketing strategy that emphasizes customer value, teamwork, and adaptability.

Important Agile Marketing Principles:

The Agile Manifesto served as the inspiration for agile marketing, which is based on the following fundamental ideas:

Agile marketing prioritizes customer-centricity, putting the client at the core of all initiatives. Meeting client wants and preferences is the main objective, and decision-making and priority are influenced by this focus.

Cross-Functional Collaboration: Agile marketing promotes the collaboration of teams with a range of talents from different departments to collaborate on marketing campaigns. This partnership encourages originality and comprehensive thinking.

Iterative and Incremental Work: Marketing initiatives are divided into more manageable, smaller components that can be finished in brief bursts. This gradual strategy enables value delivery and rapid adaption.

Data-Driven Decision-Making: Agile marketing makes decisions based on analytics and data. Marketing plans and optimizations are guided by metrics and customer feedback.

Constant Improvement: Learning and constant improvement are valued in the agile marketing philosophy. Teams evaluate their work on a regular basis, look for areas where it may be improved, and make the necessary adjustments.

Using Agile Marketing Principles:

The following crucial actions can be taken by firms to apply agile principles in marketing:

Cultural Shift: Agile marketing necessitates a change in mindset that values adaptation, change, and the needs of the client. Support from the leadership is essential to advancing this cultural shift.

Create cross-functional marketing teams by assembling people from various departments and specializations. When members of a team with different skill sets work together, creativity and problem-solving are improved.

Customer Persona Development: To comprehend the needs, preferences, and behaviors of your customers, create thorough customer personas. Content production and marketing strategies are informed by these personalities.

Prioritize your marketing tasks, concepts, and campaigns by creating a backlog and ranking them according to the worth of your customers and your company's objectives. The product backlog functions as a dynamic list that changes in response to priorities and input from customers.

Sprint Planning: Organize your marketing efforts into brief, two- to four-week periods known as sprints. The team establishes clear goals for the sprint and chooses activities from the backlog according to priority during sprint planning.

Hold daily stand-up meetings to monitor progress, address issues, and make sure everyone is on the same page regarding the goals of the sprint.

Sprint Review: Evaluate the outcomes of the work accomplished by conducting a sprint review at the conclusion of each sprint. This evaluation enables the collection of feedback and offers an example of the tasks that have been done.

Hold a retrospective following the sprint review to discuss what went well, what needs to be improved, and how to boost productivity and teamwork in the following sprint.

Data Collection and Analysis: To help with decision-making and tweaking, collect and evaluate customer input on marketing campaigns on a continual basis. Make the most of these information to improve your marketing plans.

Advantages of Using Agile Concepts in Marketing:

There are several advantages for companies and marketing teams when agile principles are implemented in marketing. Among the principal benefits are:

Flexibility and Adaptability: Marketing teams can react swiftly to shifting consumer preferences, market conditions, and new trends thanks to agile marketing. It makes it possible to react quickly to unanticipated possibilities and difficulties.

consumer-Centric Approach: Agile marketing makes sure that marketing activities are in line with the target audience by giving priority to consumer wants and preferences. This leads to more successful campaigns.

Enhanced Cooperation: Cross-functional groups work together more successfully, which promotes innovation and a comprehensive approach to marketing.

Enhanced insight: Agile marketing techniques assist team members stay in sync by offering insight into project status, task ownership, and anticipated results.

Faster Value Delivery: Teams are able to produce value in smaller, faster cycles because marketing activities are divided into manageable chunks.

Improved Risk Management: Agile marketing minimizes the risk of allocating money to initiatives that might not be well-received by consumers by promoting iterative progress and feedback.

Enhanced Employee Engagement: When workers can see the results of their efforts and are given the chance to offer suggestions and comments on marketing tactics, they become more involved.

Data-Driven Decision-Making: Agile marketing makes decisions based on feedback and data, so marketing plans are supported by insights rather than conjecture.

Difficulties in Marketing Application of Agile Principles:

Despite all of its advantages, adopting agile marketing can be difficult. Typical difficulties include:

Cultural Shift: Converting to agile marketing from traditional marketing may encounter opposition. It could be difficult at first for team members used to established procedures to adjust to new working methods.

Resource Restrictions: Investing in technology, software, and training may be necessary in order to build an agile marketing team. To meet the demands of the team, organizations must carefully distribute their resources.

Management and Leadership: Managing an agile marketing team requires strong leadership. The performance of the team may be hampered by inexperienced or unprepared leadership.

Control and Autonomy: It might be difficult to strike a balance between the requirement for supervision and control and the autonomy of the team. Companies need to strike the correct balance between allowing teams to innovate and upholding company standards and goals.

Example from the Real World: HubSpot's Agile Transition

Leading provider of inbound marketing and sales software, HubSpot, started an agile transformation journey to enhance its responsiveness and marketing procedures. They embraced agile concepts, including data-driven decision-making, cross-functional teams, and customer centricity. Consequently, HubSpot accomplished:

Enhanced marketing campaigns that prioritize the value of the customer. improved teamwork that results in creative solutions and tactics
.

a continuous learning and development culture that includes data analysis and retrospectives on a regular basis.

Improved communication and openness throughout the company.
With better results and a more responsive marketing organization, agile principles may be successfully applied to marketing, as demonstrated by HubSpot's agile transformation.

Organizations may prioritize client requirements and adjust to the ever-changing business landscape by implementing agile principles into their marketing strategy. Agile marketing allows teams to deliver more effective campaigns and react rapidly to changes in the market by encouraging a culture of flexibility, cross-functional collaboration, and continuous improvement. Although there are some difficulties along the way, implementing agile concepts in marketing has far more advantages than disadvantages. Agile marketing is a success road map that enables businesses to prosper and maintain their competitiveness in a time of fast change and changing client expectations.

Chapter 4: Adapting to Rapid Changes in the Digital Landscape.

Strategies for Success in Adapting to Quick Changes in the Digital Landscape

The digital world is a dynamic, constantly changing field that has a significant impact on how businesses, industries, and people live and work. Maintaining relevance and competitiveness in the digital sphere is difficult given the constant release of new technology, changing consumer habits, and developing online distribution channels. To succeed, organizations need to adjust to these quick changes in the digital landscape. This essay will look at the difficulties presented by the ever-changing digital landscape, how to deal with these changes, and actual cases of businesses that have made it through the digital transition successfully.

The Changing Digital Environment:

The rapidly evolving digital landscape is a result of several variables, such as market trends, legislative developments, consumer behavior shifts, and technology improvements. The following are some of the main causes of the changing digital landscape:

Emerging Technologies: New technologies are constantly upending established business paradigms and opening doors for innovation. Examples of these include blockchain, augmented reality (AR), artificial intelligence (AI), and the Internet of Things (IoT).

Consumer Behavior: Due to the ever-increasing need for tailored experiences, social media trends, mobile device usage, and other variables, consumer tastes and behaviors are always changing.

Market Competition: Startups and new entrants are posing a serious threat to existing firms in the digital domain. In order to be competitive, businesses need to adjust to shifting market conditions.

Regulatory Changes: New laws and regulations, like the GDPR, are being implemented globally by governments and regulatory organizations. These laws and regulations have an impact on how businesses function and manage customer data.

Cybersecurity Threats: Organizations must be alert and make significant investments in security measures due to the abundance of cybersecurity threats and vulnerabilities in the digital ecosystem.

Content Consumption Habits: With the emergence of podcasts, video streaming, and other media formats, people's habits for consuming content have changed, necessitating the development of new approaches to content production and delivery.

Difficulties in Quickly Adjusting to Changes:

For enterprises and organizations, adjusting to the swift changes in the digital realm poses a number of challenges:

Resource Restrictions: Staying current with emerging technologies and trends can be resource-intensive, necessitating expenditures on infrastructure, software, and staff training.

Competitive Pressure: It takes constant innovation and a proactive response to market dynamics to stay ahead of the competition in a digital landscape that is changing quickly.

Data Privacy Concerns: Stricter laws requiring ever-more-detailed compliance are a source of concern for organizations that fail to comply.

Reduced Technology Lifecycles: Due to the rapid advancement of technology, many digital solutions now have shorter lifecycles, necessitating more regular refreshes and upgrades of an organization's technology stack.

Cybersecurity Risks: Organizations must implement strong cybersecurity safeguards to safeguard sensitive data and systems as the digital world and threats change with it.

Techniques for Quick Change Adaptation:

In order to prosper in the rapidly evolving digital terrain, entities may utilize an assortment of tactics:

Accept Continuous Learning: Promote a culture of ongoing education and career advancement among staff members. Give employees access to materials and training so they can stay current on new trends and technologies.

Remain Agile: Integrate agile approaches into the culture of your company. Agile methodologies facilitate adaptability, iterative development, and speedy response to shifts in the digital environment.

Keep an Eye on Trends: Keep a regular eye on market dynamics, emerging technology, and industry trends. Through conferences, trade journals, and peer networking, stay informed.

Invest in Innovation: Provide funds for research and development, encouraging an innovative culture within the company. Create a mechanism for gathering and assessing fresh concepts.

Make decisions based on data: Utilize data to inform your decisions. Utilize analytics and insights to modify plans of action in response to performance data obtained in real time.

Work Together with Experts: Assist those in the technology and business sectors who can offer advice on navigating the digital terrain. Innovative tactics and solutions can result from cooperative efforts.

Compliance and Security: Give cybersecurity and data privacy top priority. To protect consumer data, make sure rules are followed and strong security measures are put in place.

Customer-Centric Approach: Give the client priority. Utilize data and feedback to improve goods, services, and marketing tactics, making them more suited to the demands of your target market.

Examples of Digital Adaptation in the Real World:

Netflix: Netflix is an excellent illustration of a business that has effectively adjusted to the quick changes occurring in the digital space. Netflix changed its focus from being a DVD rental service to a massive streaming platform. They were able to maintain their lead in the rapidly evolving streaming market by embracing new technology and making investments in the production of unique content.

Amazon: By growing its offerings and using cutting-edge technologies, Amazon consistently adjusts to the changing digital environment. They have made investments in AI-powered customer interactions, smart home appliances, and drone delivery. They remain at the forefront of e-commerce because to their customer-centric strategy.

Tesla: The company's inventiveness in developing electric cars and autonomous driving technologies is credited with its success. To remain competitive in the automotive business, they have embraced agile development principles and are always updating the software in their vehicles.

Facebook: Facebook began as a social networking site and has now grown into a digital empire. They've made investments in AI and VR while also acquiring Oculus, WhatsApp, and Instagram. Facebook adjusts by keeping on the cutting edge of emerging technology and media.

Airbnb: By responding to customer demands for distinctive and local experiences, Airbnb upended the travel sector. They established a worldwide sharing economy by utilizing the potential of internet platforms and user-generated content.

Businesses and organizations hoping to prosper in the modern day must be able to quickly adjust to changes in the digital landscape. Although there are many obstacles in this changing world, they can be overcome with the right tactics. Businesses that prioritize customer-centricity, agility, data-driven decision-making, and continuous learning will be more successful navigating the rapidly changing digital landscape. Organizations may not only adapt to the digital transformation, but also lead it by putting money into innovation, being diligent about security and compliance, and working with specialists. In the digital age, companies such as Netflix, Amazon, Tesla, Facebook, and Airbnb are real-life examples of the benefits of embracing change and innovation. Those who grasp opportunities and overcome obstacles in the digital landscape will succeed in a world where flexibility is essential.

The Role of Data in Agile Marketing.

Data's Place in Agile Marketing: Making Knowledge-Based Decisions That Lead to Success

The lifeblood of contemporary marketing is now data. In the era of digitalization, marketers may gain priceless insights into client behavior, preferences, and the efficacy of their campaigns thanks to the massive amount of data generated through online interactions. Data is central to decision-making in agile marketing, a dynamic approach that prioritizes flexibility and ongoing development. The importance of data in agile marketing, how it shapes strategies and tactics, and the advantages it offers marketing teams will all be discussed in this essay.

Data's Importance in Agile Marketing

Although data has always been crucial to marketing, in the era of digital marketing, its significance has grown considerably. It is essential to several facets of agile marketing, including:

Customer insights: Data offers a thorough grasp of the demographics, inclinations, and behavior of customers. Marketers are able to develop more relevant and customized advertising because to these insights.

Performance Metrics: By monitoring key performance indicators (KPIs) like conversion rates, click-through rates, and return on investment (ROI), data may be used to assess the efficacy of marketing initiatives.

Continuous Improvement: Data is used by agile marketing to pinpoint areas that need to be improved. Marketers can improve their results by modifying their strategy and methods through routine data analysis.

Adaptability: Data gives marketers the ability to respond swiftly to shifts in the competitive environment, consumer behavior, or the market. Agile marketing teams use data to guide their decisions and adjust course as needed.

Customer input: Customer input, which frequently takes the form of social media interactions, online reviews, and comments, offers insightful qualitative data that can influence marketing plans and new product development.

How Agile Marketing Strategies Are Informed by Data:

Customer Personas: A thorough grasp of the target market is the first step in agile marketing. Marketers can better target certain segments with their messaging and campaigns by using data to build comprehensive consumer profiles.

Agile marketing teams use real-time data to inform their decision-making. With A/B testing, for instance, marketers can test various iterations of an advertisement or campaign to see which works best.

Iterative Campaigns: Agile marketing teams learn what is and isn't working using data-driven insights. Iterative campaign development is made possible by this feedback loop, where adjustments are made in response to data analysis.

Content Optimization: Data is used by marketers to identify the kinds of content that appeal to their target audience the most. These could be in the form of infographics, movies, blogs, or other media.

Budget Allocation: Data facilitates more efficient resource allocation for marketers. They are able to modify their budget allocation based on the channels that are yielding the highest return on investment.

Advantages of Agile Marketing Driven by Data:

Enhanced Campaign Performance: Agile marketing teams may optimize their campaigns for maximum impact by utilizing data to fine-tune them. Through constant analysis and optimization, they can attain superior outcomes.

Higher Customer Satisfaction: Customers respond better to tailored marketing initiatives that are based on data-driven insights, which raises customer satisfaction and engagement.

Improved Resource Allocation: Agile marketing teams can focus on the channels and strategies that produce the best outcomes in order to deploy their resources more effectively.

Faster Adaptation to Change: Being able to quickly adjust is a huge advantage in the ever-changing digital landscape. Agile marketing teams can make well-informed judgments when market conditions change thanks to data.

Accountability and Transparency: Data-driven marketing facilitates team accountability by offering transparency into campaign performance. Marketers are able to observe which techniques are working and which ones require tweaking.

Cost savings: Agile marketing teams can cut costs by reducing wasteful spending by leveraging data to optimize campaigns and distribute resources sensibly.

Data-Driven Agile Marketing's Challenges:

Although data is an effective instrument in agile marketing, it presents a unique set of difficulties:

Data Overload: There is often too much data available. Finding the most important insights requires marketers to sort through a ton of data.

Data Quality: Only very accurate and high-quality data may be put to any use. Marketers must make sure the information they gather is accurate and pertinent.

Privacy Concerns: As data privacy becomes more and more important, marketers need to manage a complicated web of laws and customer expectations while gathering and utilizing data.

Technology Integration: It might be difficult to integrate data from different tools and sources. To expedite this process, marketers might need to make investments in data management solutions.

Requirements for Skill: A certain level of proficiency in data analysis and interpretation is necessary for data-driven marketing. Not every member of the marketing team might have these abilities.

Real-Life Illustrations:

Netflix: One business that makes extensive use of data-driven marketing is Netflix. Utilizing user data, the streaming behemoth makes personalized show thumbnails, suggests material, and even develops original series according to viewer tastes.

Amazon: Amazon enhances the shopping experience and boosts sales by using user data to create personalized recommendations and offers. To generate these suggestions, they examine past browsing and purchasing activity as well as the amount of time spent on product pages.

Spotify: Spotify uses user data to generate customized playlists and make music recommendations. Their algorithms examine each user's listening tastes and behaviors to create the ideal playlists.

Airbnb: Data is used by Airbnb to improve pricing suggestions, search algorithm performance, and user experience in general. They continuously improve their platform by looking at data on bookings, host and guest behavior, and market demand.

Agile marketing relies heavily on data to inform strategy, make decisions, and optimize campaigns. Data offers organizations the insights they need to remain flexible and adaptable in a digital environment marked by fast change and intense competition. Agile marketing teams may create more individualized, successful campaigns, swiftly adjust to changes in the market, spend resources effectively, and ultimately produce better outcomes by utilizing data. The advantages of data-driven marketing, which include enhanced campaign performance, higher consumer happiness, and cost savings, greatly exceed the drawbacks. Empirical instances from businesses such as Netflix, Amazon, Spotify, and Airbnb demonstrate the revolutionary potential of data in agile marketing. Agile marketing will continue to be a crucial tactic for success as the digital world changes, and data's importance in marketing will only grow.

Leveraging Data Analytics and Market Insights.

Using Market Insights and Data Analytics to Uncover the Power of Well-Informed Decision-Making

Utilizing data analytics and market insights has become a critical tactic for companies looking to stay competitive and make wise decisions in today's data-driven environment. Data analytics is more than just gathering statistics; it's also about deriving insightful conclusions, seeing patterns, and comprehending customer behavior. When mixed with market insights, organizations receive a whole picture of their target market and sector. We will examine the importance of data analytics and market insights, their complementary roles, and the significant effects they can have on an organization's performance in this essay.

The Potential of Analytical Data

Analyzing data sets to find significant trends, patterns, and insights is known as data analytics. It uses a variety of methods, ranging from sophisticated machine learning algorithms to fundamental statistical analysis. Within the context of business, data analytics performs multiple vital roles:

Data-Driven Decision Making: The basis for well-informed decision-making is provided by data analytics. Organizations can make evidence-based, as opposed to just intuitive, strategic decisions by examining both historical and current data.

Performance Evaluation: Companies can use data analytics to evaluate how well different parts of their business—like marketing initiatives, product development, and customer support—are performing.

Cost Reduction: By using data analysis to find inefficiencies and wasteful areas, costs can be decreased and resources can be allocated more effectively.

Competitive Advantage: Businesses who use data analytics to their advantage have a competitive advantage. They can anticipate client demands, respond quickly to changes in the market, and surpass competitors.

Customer insights: Businesses may comprehend the preferences, actions, and buying patterns of their customers by analyzing their data. This knowledge is crucial for focusing marketing campaigns and providing individualized service.

Market Analysis:

A deeper comprehension of the external environment in which a firm functions is encompassed by market insights. This entails being aware of market trends, rivalry, customer inclinations, and legislative modifications. Market insights are crucial since they let businesses do the following:

Keep Up: Companies can proactively address changes and disruptions by keeping an eye on industry developments. They remain ahead of rivals who might take longer to adjust because of this.

Identify Opportunities: Market research reveals new avenues for business expansion through the provision of additional goods and services.

Risk Mitigation: Organizations can plan for and lessen any negative effects by having a clear understanding of market risks, such as recessions or changes in customer attitude.

Competitive Analysis: Keeping one's edge in the market requires modifying one's own strategy based on an analysis of competitors' tactics and results.

Customer-Centricity: Providing a customer-centric experience requires having a thorough understanding of the preferences and behavior of your customers within the larger market context.

The Combination of Market Insights with Data Analytics:

Market insights and data analytics work best together. By delving deeply into an organization's internal data, data analytics offers detailed insights into its business processes and contacts with customers. Contrarily, market insights adopt a wider perspective and take into account outside variables that may have an impact on the company. The combination of these two factors produces a comprehensive understanding that enables companies to prosper. This is how they collaborate:

Data-Driven Market Insights: Organizations can make inferences about consumer behavior and market trends by examining both internal and external data. For instance, they can determine how market changes affect consumer preferences by comparing client data with patterns observed across the industry.

Competitive Analysis: Organizations can do competitive analysis from a comprehensive standpoint by fusing data analytics with market insights. They are able to comprehend the acts of their rivals as well as the reactions of their clientele.

Customer-Centricity: Market insights provide a wider context for the detailed customer insights obtained via data analytics. Knowing how their customer-centric initiatives fit into the broader market landscape helps firms to refine them.

Opportunity Identification: Market insights can assist firms in assessing how these prospects match with wider industry trends, and data analytics can reveal hidden potential within a company's operations.

Risk mitigation: Data analytics enables firms to evaluate how prepared they are to face market hazards, while market insights offer early warning signs about such dangers. Organizations can also benefit from data analytics by predicting and measuring the effects of possible market risks.

Using Market Insights and Data Analytics to Your Advantage

Well-Informed Decision-Making: Companies use more thoughtful tactics and rely less on intuition when making judgments.

Competitive Edge: Businesses can outperform their rivals by quickly adjusting to changes in the market and having a deeper understanding of their clientele.

Resource Efficiency: By using data-driven insights, businesses may optimize processes and reduce costs by allocating resources more effectively.

Risk management: Data analytics and market insights combine to assist firms in identifying and successfully reducing market risks.

Better Product Development: More successful product or service development might result from a thorough grasp of consumer demands and market dynamics.

Obstacles & Things to Think About:

There are obstacles when using market insights and data analytics:

Data Quality: It is essential that the data utilized for analysis be of a high quality. Deficient or erroneous information may result in poor decision-making.

Privacy and Compliance: Businesses need to make sure they are in compliance with legislation like the CCPA and GDPR as well as manage data privacy requirements.

Data Integration: Effective data integration and management are necessary when combining internal and external data sources, which can be a technically difficult task.

Skills Gap: For successful implementation, proficient data analysts and market researchers are necessary. Companies might have to spend money on expert hiring or training.

Cost: Although the potential return on investment frequently justifies the costs, implementing data analytics and market insights tools and processes can be expensive.

Real-Life Illustrations:

Amazon: Amazon monitors what customers view and buy on its e-commerce platform by using data analytics to track customer behavior. Additionally, it makes use of market intelligence to predict consumer preferences and e-commerce trends.

Netflix: To provide its consumers with personalized content recommendations, Netflix uses data analytics. It can better grasp how the entertainment sector is changing and maintain its leadership position in the streaming market thanks to market analytics.

Spotify: To determine what music listeners listen to and when, Spotify uses data analytics. It uses market knowledge to predict consumer preferences for various genres and trends in the music industry.

McDonald's: Based on consumer preferences and market insights into shifting dietary patterns and trends in the fast-food sector, McDonald's uses data analytics to optimize menu offerings.

It is imperative for businesses to use data analytics and market insights if they want to succeed in the ever-changing business environment of today. Businesses may remain ahead of the competition, allocate resources effectively, manage risks, and make data-driven decisions thanks to the synergy between data analytics and market insights. It's a way to not just succeed but also to change and grow in a world that's always changing. Empirical instances from major players in the market, such as Amazon, Netflix, Spotify, and McDonald's, highlight how revolutionary this strategy can be. Organizations that adeptly utilize these insights will be well-positioned to spearhead their respective industries and satisfy their clientele's demands as data and industry dynamics persistently change.

Navigating the World of Social Media and Influencer Marketing.

Getting Around in the Social Media and Influencer Marketing World: Successful Strategies

Social media and influencer marketing are now essential parts of any comprehensive marketing plan in the digital age. These platforms give companies the chance to engage with their target market, increase brand recognition, and foster brand loyalty. But mastering the realms of influencer marketing and social media is no easy task. It calls for a strong grasp of the dynamic environment, practical approaches, and a dedication to genuineness. We will discuss the importance of social media and influencer marketing in this article, as well as important success tactics and the opportunities and problems these platforms offer.

Social Media and Influencer Marketing's Significance

Social media platforms have completely changed how businesses and individuals interact with their audience, share information, and communicate. Several important elements highlight the importance of social media and influencer marketing:

Broad Reach: With billions of consumers actively using social media platforms, businesses may reach a huge worldwide audience.

Targeted Advertising: Social media platforms provide businesses with powerful options for targeting particular interests, demographics, and behavioral patterns.

material Sharing: Through the active sharing of articles, films, and other types of material on social media, marketers are able to reach a wider audience by utilizing user-generated content.

Engagement of Customers: Social media platforms offer a direct channel of communication with consumers, encouraging interaction, comments, and allegiance.

Influencer Power: Influencer marketing makes use of people who have a sizable online following to help firms gain access to their authority and audience.

Data and Analytics: Businesses may evaluate the results of their marketing campaigns and make data-driven decisions by utilizing the data and analytics capabilities that social media platforms offer.

Essential Techniques for Influencer and Social Media Marketing Success:

Know Your Audience: Effective social media and influencer marketing are built on a solid understanding of your target market. To determine the demographics, inclinations, and behaviors of your audience, conduct market research.

Select the Correct Platforms: Social networking sites are not made equal. Choose media channels that complement the tastes of your target market and the essence of your business. For instance, whereas Twitter is a text-based site, Instagram and Pinterest are visual.

Consistent Branding: Make sure your voice and image are the same on all of your social media platforms. Building a strong and recognizable brand identity is aided by this.

Produce Useful stuff: Provide your readers with useful stuff. Content should align with the interests of your audience, whether it takes the shape of educational blog pieces, entertaining videos, or motivational photos.

Utilize Influencers: Find influencers whose fan base is similar to your intended market. Work together to really market your goods and services.

Interact with Your Audience: Answer messages and comments, promote conversations, and convey that you appreciate their opinions.

Paid Advertising: To target particular demographics and raise your profile, make use of the paid advertising choices provided by social media networks.

Utilize Analytics: Using the platforms' analytics capabilities, keep a frequent eye on your social media performance. Examine what is effective and modify your plan of action accordingly.

Develop Relationships: The goal of influencer marketing should be to establish sincere connections with influencers. Campaigns with genuine partnerships are more successful.

Opportunities and Difficulties:

Influencer marketing and social media provide a lot of benefits, but they also come with a number of drawbacks.

Problems:

Algorithm Updates: The reach and exposure of your material may be affected by the regular algorithm updates made by social media networks.

Saturation: It can be difficult to stand out from the crowd on social media due to its saturation. Your writing ought to be captivating and original.

Negative Comments: PR disasters or unfavorable comments can be amplified on social media. Companies must be ready to handle and resolve problems quickly.

Costs: Influencer marketing can come at a lot of different prices, as some influencers have hefty charge structures. It might be difficult to strike the correct balance between cost and return on investment.

Authenticity: It's important to keep being authentic. Consumers are growing more perceptive and adept at identifying false or dishonest advertising.

Potentialities:

Social media networks provide businesses with precise targeting choices for targeted advertising, which enables them to reach particular demographics and interests.

Engagement: Social media gives you a direct channel of contact with your audience, allowing for mutual engagement and the development of connections.

User-Generated Content: Content created and shared by users about goods and services is a great way to spread word-of-mouth advertising.

Influencer marketing: By collaborating with influencers, companies may reach a wider audience and benefit from their reach and credibility.

Data and Analytics: Social media platforms give businesses access to data and analytics tools, enabling them to assess the success of their marketing campaigns and make informed decisions.

Real-Life Illustrations:

Coca-Cola: With millions of followers on numerous social media platforms, Coca-Cola has a sizable online presence. Their strategy of encouraging customers to share their Coca-Cola experiences has allowed them to profit from user-generated content. Personalized bottle labels with popular names were part of the "Share a Coke" campaign, which was a huge success.

Nike: To promote its products, Nike regularly works with athletes and influencers on social media and has a strong online presence in these spaces. Using a variety of athletes, their "Just Do It" campaign has shown to be an effective long-term tactic.

Huda Kattan: A well-known influencer in the cosmetics and beauty sectors, Huda Kattan is also known as Huda Beauty. She successfully partnered with cosmetic firms and developed her brand on social media, amassing a sizable fan base in the process.

Dove: Dove is well-known for its advertisements that support self-worth and body positivity. They've successfully used social media to promote dialogue on these subjects and build a strong sense of brand loyalty.

In the digital age, social media and influencer marketing are essential parts of a full marketing plan. They give companies the chance to interact with consumers, reach a large audience, and establish real connections when done well. However, caution must be used when navigating the difficulties presented by cost, authenticity, and algorithm updates. Effective social media and influencer marketing tactics necessitate a thorough comprehension of the intended audience, dependable branding, and the capacity to produce high-quality content. Increased visibility, user-generated content, and the development of genuine connections with influencers and customers can all be facilitated by these tactics. Examples from the real world include Coca-Cola, Nike, influencers like Huda Kattan, and Dove advertisements that demonstrate the significant effects these tactics may have. People who successfully manage the social media and influencer marketing landscape with sincerity and intelligence will thrive in a future where digital relationships are more crucial than ever.

Chapter 5: Measuring and Optimizing Agile Marketing Success.

Assessing and Enhancing Agile Marketing Performance: A Data-Centered Method for Ongoing Enhancement

Agile marketing has become a potent approach for companies looking to adjust to the ever-evolving demands of their clients and the market. A crucial element of agile marketing is the capacity for continuous optimization and measurement of success. Enterprises can use data analytics to track the effectiveness of marketing initiatives, make well-informed decisions, and refine their strategies in the digital age, where insights are critical and data is plentiful. This essay will examine the importance of tracking and refining agile marketing performance, the essential metrics and KPIs (Key Performance Indicators) that are involved, and the tactics for continuously improving marketing initiatives.

The Importance of Assessing and Improving Agile Marketing Performance:

Agile marketing success must be measured and optimized for a number of reasons.

Data-Driven Decisions: Data and insights are the foundation of agile marketing. Marketing teams may make better judgments and hone their strategies with the support of regular data assessment and analysis.

Constant Improvement: Iteration is a fundamental component of agile marketing. Teams can find areas for improvement in campaign performance, audience engagement, or resource allocation by measuring success.

Resource Efficiency: Businesses may maximize the impact of their marketing budget and minimize waste by tracking the effectiveness of their marketing initiatives.

Adaptability: In a market that is changing frequently, the ability to gauge success and make timely adjustments to plans based on data is crucial. Teams using agile marketing are able to adjust as the market changes.

Goal Alignment: Success measurement makes sure that marketing initiatives are in line with the overarching objectives of the company. It aids groups in staying on course and pursuing common goals.

Important KPIs & Metrics in Agile Marketing:

Organizations must monitor a variety of crucial measures and KPIs in order to assess and maximize the success of agile marketing, including:

Customer Acquisition Cost (CAC): This measure helps businesses assess how effectively they are using their marketing budget by estimating the cost of bringing on a new client.

Customer Lifetime Value (CLV): CLV calculates a customer's long-term value and helps businesses focus their marketing efforts on acquiring high-value clients.

Conversion Rate: The percentage of website visitors who complete a desired activity, like subscribing to a newsletter or making a purchase, is monitored by this statistic.

Churn Rate: Churn rate is a metric used by corporations to determine which areas require customer retention initiatives. It quantifies the rate at which consumers discontinue using a product or service.

Click-Through Rate (CTR): This metric expresses the proportion of users that click on a particular link in an email or web page. It is useful for determining how successful calls to action are.

Return on Investment (ROI): ROI compares the revenue earned (return on investment) to the marketing spend (investment) in order to assess the profitability of marketing initiatives.

Social Media involvement: The impact and level of involvement of social media campaigns are measured by metrics such as likes, shares, comments, and retweets.

Email Marketing Metrics: In order to gauge the success of their email communications, businesses can use open, click, and conversion rates in their campaigns.

Organic Search Traffic: Tracking organic search volume, together with keyword performance and search engine ranks, helps evaluate the effectiveness of SEO campaigns.

Net Promoter Score (NPS) and Customer Satisfaction: These metrics gauge how satisfied consumers are generally and how likely they are to refer the product or service to others.

Methods for Assessing and Improving Agile Marketing Performance:

Establish Clear Objectives: Setting clear objectives is the first step towards successful agile marketing. What particular objectives does a marketing campaign or initiative have? Determining these objectives will direct the measurement process.

Employ Data Analytics technologies: Companies must use data analytics technologies to efficiently gather and analyze data in order to gauge their success. Important information can be gained via tools like Google Analytics, Adobe Analytics, and many marketing automation platforms.

Frequent Reporting and Monitoring: To track the effectiveness of marketing campaigns, set up a frequent reporting plan. This could be done on a daily, weekly, or monthly basis, based on the goals and nature of the campaign.

A/B testing compares two variations of a marketing element (such as a landing page, ad copy, or email subject line) to see which works better. This method aids in optimizing components for optimal impact.

Customer Feedback and Surveys: Direct customer feedback can be gathered via questionnaires and surveys, which can yield qualitative data to support quantitative measurements.

Analyze your competitors' performance by comparing it to theirs in your sector. This can assist in determining the areas in which you must develop in order to stay competitive.

Campaign Development Iteratively: Agile marketing is an iterative process. Utilize the information you gather to continuously improve your efforts. Adapt in light of new information to enhance outcomes over time.

Adjust to Market Shifts: The marketing environment is always changing. Utilize data to quickly adjust to new trends and changes in the market.

Employee Training and Skill Development: Make sure the members of your marketing team possess the abilities and know-how required for efficient data measurement and analysis. Upskilling or training may be required for this.

Invest in Marketing Technology: Make an investment in technology that makes gathering, analyzing, and optimizing data easier. Numerous marketing automation systems come with tools for gauging performance.

Difficulties in Assessing and Improving Agile Marketing Performance:

Data Quality: Data dependability and correctness are crucial. Deficient or erroneous information may result in poor decision-making.

Data Privacy and Compliance: Businesses need to make sure they are in compliance with legislation such as the CCPA and GDPR, as well as manage data privacy requirements.

Resource Allocation: It can be difficult to allocate the appropriate resources for data analysis and optimization. Additional tools and technology, or a dedicated staff, might be needed for this.

Requirements for Skill: Effective measurement and optimization require highly skilled data analysts and marketers. Companies might have to spend money on expert hiring or training.

Costs: Putting data analytics tools and procedures into place can be expensive, but the potential return on investment frequently makes the cost worthwhile.

Real-Life Illustrations:

HubSpot: HubSpot is a sales and marketing software provider that provides a full range of inbound marketing solutions, such as reporting and data analytics. They assist companies in gauging the effectiveness of their marketing campaigns and refining their plans in light of data-driven insights.

Airbnb: To gauge the effectiveness of its marketing initiatives and adjust to shifts in the travel sector, Airbnb use data analytics. They examine booking patterns and client information to refine their pricing tactics.

Zappos: To gauge customer success and pleasure, the online shoe and apparel shop use a data-driven methodology. To continuously improve the customer experience, they keep an eye on measures like NPS and customer feedback.

In today's data-driven environment, measuring and optimizing agile marketing success is essential. Businesses are better able to adjust, compete, and prosper in a market that is changing quickly when they make an investment in success measurement, use data analytics, and apply insights to maximize their marketing efforts. Because marketing is agile, it necessitates regular reporting, A/B testing, a thorough grasp of important metrics and KPIs, and a dedication to continual improvement. Even though there are obstacles, the advantages of wise choices, effective use of resources, and flexibility make the work valuable. Empirical instances from businesses such as HubSpot, Airbnb, and Zappos demonstrate the significant influence of a data-driven marketing strategy. Success and sustained expansion are in store for those that use data wisely as the marketing environment changes over time.

Setting Clear Objectives and Key Results (OKRs).

Clearly Defined Goals and Key Results (OKRs): A Route to Success and Enhancing Output

Establishing well-defined goals and crucial outcomes, or OKRs, is an effective structure that can benefit both individuals and companies. OKRs offer a methodical way to set objectives, track advancement, and produce outcomes. This approach, which has been made popular by businesses like Intel and Google, is crucial for improving team alignment, performance, and the development of a continuous improvement culture. This essay will discuss the importance of establishing specific goals and critical outcomes, the components of the OKR framework, and effective implementation techniques.

The Importance of Specifying Specific Goals and Important Outcomes:

It is crucial to establish specific goals and outcomes for multiple reasons.

Alignment: OKRs facilitate individual and team alignment with the overarching organizational objectives. Synergy is improved when all parties are aware of the main goals and their responsibilities in accomplishing them.

Focus: OKRs remove uncertainty and guarantee that efforts are focused on the most important tasks by precisely outlining what needs to be accomplished and tracking progress.

Accountability is encouraged by the OKRs' transparency. Individual and group performance are the team members' responsibility, which can inspire dedication and drive.

Adaptability: OKRs facilitate adaptability and flexibility. Objectives and important outcomes might be modified in response to shifts in the market or in priorities.

Constant Improvement: OKRs' cyclical structure promotes constant improvement. Over time, improved performance is the result of regular assessments and modifications.

Components of the Framework for OKR:

The two main components of the OKR framework are the objectives and key results.

1. Purpose:

Objectives are succinct, unambiguous explanations of what has to be done. They usually have a sense of purpose and direction, are motivating and ambitious. The question "What do we want to achieve?" should be addressed by the objectives, which should be clear and qualitative.
2. Major Findings:

Key Results are precise, quantifiable, and time-bound benchmarks that show how close the goals are to being met. "How will we know we've achieved the objective?" is the question they address. Key Results function as numerical measurements that enable the quantification of success.
Key Findings ought to be:

Measurable: They must have a quantitative expression. "Increase website traffic by 20%," for instance, can be measured, while "Improve website traffic" cannot.

Time-bound: The accomplishment of Key Results ought to be subject to a set amount of time. For example, "Grow social media following by 10% within the upcoming quarter" gives a precise date.

Particulars: The main findings must to be clear-cut and accurate. Avert ambiguous or excessively broad metrics. Progress tracking requires clarity.

Achievable: Although the Objectives ought to be lofty, the Key Results ought to be practical and doable in the allotted time.

Aligned: The accomplishment of the Objective should be directly impacted by the Key Results. They ought to help achieve and forward the main objective.

Applying OKRs in a Successful Way:

To properly implement OKRs, there are several phases and recommended practices to follow:

Clarity and Simplicity: Make sure that OKRs are unambiguous and simple. Refrain from giving them undue information and complexity. Everyone can grasp and support them more readily when they are made simpler.

Make sure everything is aligned from top to bottom. Teams' and individuals' OKRs should be influenced by the organizational goals. Everyone ought to understand how their efforts further the larger goal.

Frequent Check-Ins: Arrange frequent check-ins to assess OKR progress. Regular evaluations make it easier to remember the objectives and enable last-minute modifications as necessary.

Transparency: Allow each team member to see the OKRs. Accountability is aided and a sense of shared responsibility is fostered by transparency.

Select a Variety of Goals: Mixing the goals in a balanced way. Incorporate both more realistic goals that guarantee progress is being made and aspirational ones that drive the team to new heights.

Continuous Improvement: OKRs ought to be reviewed and modified on a regular basis. Although a quarterly cadence is typical, organizational needs and the nature of the objectives will determine how frequently this occurs.

Ownership: Clearly identify the people or groups in charge of every Key Outcome. Possession guarantees that someone is responsible for advancing the cause.

Encourage an environment where feedback and flexibility are valued. Promote frank discussion on the OKR process's strengths and areas for development.

Implementing OKRs presents challenges.

There are certain obstacles to overcome while implementing OKRs:

Excessively Ambitious Goals: If your goals are constantly out of reach, they may cause demotivation and even burnout.

Lack of Clarity: Team members may find it difficult to comprehend their part in accomplishing OKRs if they are not explained well enough or if they are overly complicated.

Neglecting Key Results: Vague or immeasurable goals might come from concentrating just on objectives and ignoring the key results.

Opposition to Change: Team members accustomed to using conventional goal-setting techniques may oppose the adoption of an OKR-based system.

Inconsistent Implementation: Within the organization, inconsistent implementation can cause misalignment and misunderstanding.

Real-Life Illustrations:

Google: OKRs are frequently attributed to Google. Throughout the organization, OKRs are widely used. A Google OKR would read something like this: "Key Result: Increase click-through rate by 15% in the next quarter; Objective: Improve the user experience on the search page."

Intel: OKRs have been successfully implemented by Intel for many years. An instance might be "Objective: Strengthen our market position in the semiconductor industry; Key Result: Increase market share by 2% by the end of the fiscal year."

LinkedIn: OKRs are now used by LinkedIn for goal-setting. An instance may be "Objective: Enhance user engagement; Key Result: Increase weekly active users by 10% in the next three months."

A process called setting clear objectives and key outcomes (OKRs) gives individuals and organizations the ability to set objectives, track their progress, and improve performance. It encourages accountability, clarity, alignment, flexibility, and ongoing development. Organizations may make sure they are on track to meet their goals by decomposing objectives into quantifiable key results. Effective OKR implementation necessitates transparency, alignment, simplicity, frequent check-ins, and a feedback-friendly culture. Although there may be obstacles in the form of opposition to change or overly ambitious goals, the advantages of OKRs in terms of attention, alignment, and outcomes greatly exceed these drawbacks. The practical applicability of OKRs in promoting success and performance is demonstrated by real-world examples from organizations such as Google, Intel, and LinkedIn. Setting and completing goals is essential in today's society, and the OKR framework offers a methodical route to excellence and ongoing development.

Data-Driven Decision-Making.

Data-Driven Decision-Making: Unlocking Information's Potential to Make Better Decisions

Data-driven decision-making has emerged as a crucial tactic for both individuals and companies in today's data-rich environment. Making decisions based on data and insights is critical in all areas of life, including business, government, healthcare, and personal relationships. This strategy makes use of information to improve decision quality and accuracy, reduce risk, and promote success. This essay will examine the importance of data-driven decision-making, its guiding principles and advantages, as well as implementation best practices and obstacles.

The Importance of Making Decisions Based on Data:

Decisions based on data are extremely important for the following reasons:

Precision and Accuracy: Evidence-based decisions derived from data lessen the dependence on conjecture and gut feeling. More precise and accurate decisions are made as a result.

Objective Insights: Data are impartial and unbiased. It guarantees that choices are made on the basis of objective facts rather than arbitrary judgments and gets rid of personal prejudices.

Efficiency: Making decisions can be done more quickly and effectively when data is used. Decision-making can be expedited and new insights can be obtained fast through data analysis.

Risk Mitigation: Data gives organizations the ability to recognize and evaluate possible risks, guiding their decision-making to reduce unfavorable consequences.

Competitive Advantage: Businesses with efficient data use have an advantage over their rivals. They may beat rivals, foresee client demands, and react quickly to changes in the market.

Important Guidelines for Making Data-Driven Decisions:

Data-driven decision-making is predicated on a number of essential ideas:

Data collection: Compile accurate and up-to-date, pertinent, and trustworthy data from a variety of sources.

Analysis: Process and evaluate the data using analytical tools and techniques to find important patterns and insights.

Visualization: To make data easier to understand and more accessible, present it in a clear and visual way using tools like charts, graphs, and dashboards.

Continuous Learning: Adopt a mindset that is focused on ongoing development. Review and modify tactics frequently in light of data-driven findings.

Encourage cooperation between various teams and departments by fostering cross-functional teams. This guarantees the organization-wide integration of insights derived from data.

Ethical Considerations: To uphold confidence and adhere to legal requirements, make sure ethical data practices, such as privacy and security, are followed.

Advantages of Making Decisions Based on Data:

There are many advantages to making decisions based on data:

Better Decision Quality: Fact-based information forms the basis of data-driven judgments, which produce decisions of a higher caliber.

Cost Reduction: By using data analysis to find inefficiencies and wasteful areas, costs can be decreased and resources can be allocated more effectively.

Efficiency: Decisions based on data are frequently made more quickly and effectively, which cuts down on the amount of time needed to make decisions.

Competitive Edge: Businesses that successfully use data to their advantage have a competitive advantage. They can outperform rivals and respond quickly to changes in the market.

Customer insights: Businesses may comprehend the preferences, actions, and buying patterns of their customers by analyzing their data. This knowledge is crucial for focusing marketing campaigns and providing individualized service.

Difficulties in Putting Data-Driven Decision Making Into Practice:

There are difficulties in putting data-driven decision-making into practice:

Data Quality: It is essential that the data utilized for analysis be of a high quality. Deficient or erroneous information may result in poor decision-making.

Privacy and Compliance: Businesses need to make sure they are in compliance with legislation like the CCPA and GDPR as well as manage data privacy requirements.

Data Integration: It might be technically difficult to combine data from many sources; therefore, efficient data integration and management are necessary.

Skills Gap: Expert decision-makers and data analysts are necessary for successful implementation. Companies might have to spend money on expert hiring or training.

Cost: From obtaining the required tools to constructing the infrastructure and knowledge, implementing data-driven decision-making may be expensive.

Optimal Techniques for Making Data-Driven Decisions:

To optimize the advantages of data-driven decision-making, take into account following recommended practices:

Define Your Goals and Objectives Clearly: Make data-driven decisions by clearly defining your goals and objectives. Your data analysis activities will be guided by a well-defined aim.

Data Governance: To guarantee data security, quality, and regulatory compliance, put in place robust data governance procedures.

Invest in Analytics Tools: Make an investment in platforms and tools for data analytics that are appropriate for your organization's needs and objectives.

Data Visualization: To help non-technical stakeholders better understand and access complicated data, employ data visualization approaches.

Interdisciplinary Teams: To guarantee a comprehensive viewpoint, assemble interdisciplinary teams that integrate subject knowledge with data analytic abilities.

Frequent Reporting: Establish frequent cycles for reporting and data reviews to monitor developments, spot trends, and make necessary strategy adjustments.

Scalability: Make sure your data-driven decision-making procedures are adaptable enough to grow with your company and change as its demands do.

Examples of Data-Driven Decision Making in the Real World:

Netflix: Netflix makes content suggestions based on data-driven decision-making. Their ability to give tailored content recommendations based on user viewing patterns and interests has helped them succeed in the streaming market.

Amazon: For consumer suggestions and inventory management, Amazon use data-driven decision-making. Their supply chain is optimized and product suggestions are made by tracking user activity using algorithms.

Google: Google changes its search algorithm using data-driven decision-making. They employ data to raise the caliber and relevancy of search results, therefore improving the user experience.

Facebook: Facebook optimizes its advertising platform through data-driven decision-making. They give advertisers comprehensive analytics and insights so they may decide on their ad campaigns based on facts.

In the current environment, making decisions based on data has become essential rather than just a means of gaining a competitive edge. Making well-informed decisions based on data and insights has shown to be the most efficient approach to promote success, improve decision quality, and lower risks in a wide range of industries, including business, government, healthcare, and many more. In addition to gaining a competitive edge, businesses that use data-driven decision-making make sure their operations and plans are successful, economical, and in line with their objectives. Although there are obstacles to overcome, adopting data-driven decision-making has much more advantages than disadvantages. Empirical instances from prominent business players such as Netflix, Amazon, Google, and Facebook highlight the revolutionary potential of data-driven choices in attaining prosperity. Data is everywhere these days, and those who can use it to their advantage will be more successful and continue to expand.

Chapter 6: Conclusion:

Conclusion: The Influence of Constant Learning and Well-Informed Decisions

We've covered important facets of the business and marketing landscape, how agile methodologies are changing industries, how data and insights are used in decision-making, and the values that underpin effective teamwork and leadership during our journey through the various topics covered in this essay series. As we draw to a close, it's critical to consider the overarching themes that unite these topics and emphasize the value of making wise decisions and embracing lifelong learning in our constantly changing environment.

Agility and Adaptation:

Technological innovations and shifting consumer tastes have created a fast-paced business environment that necessitates agility and adaptability. The message is evident in everything from the development of marketing to the use of agile principles: people who can swiftly pivot and adapt are better suited to flourish in a dynamic environment. Businesses may remain ahead of the curve and better serve their clients' requirements by putting agile marketing approaches into practice and encouraging a collaborative, innovative society.

The Function of Data

The foundation of contemporary decision-making is data. The importance of utilizing data in market insights, data analytics, or agile marketing cannot be emphasized. It gives firms the ability to manage resources effectively, optimize strategy, and make well-informed decisions. The practical instances of data-driven businesses, such as Google, Amazon, and Netflix, highlight how transformational data can be in attaining success.

Teamwork and Leadership:

Strong teamwork and leadership are prerequisites for any successful firm. Achieving common goals requires creating agile marketing teams and encouraging an innovative and cooperative culture. The people that comprise these teams are essential to the organization's success. Within an agile marketing team, defining and developing essential responsibilities guarantees that each person's abilities are utilized to their full potential.

Constant Enhancement:

One idea that keeps coming up in these works is ongoing progress. The journey doesn't stop at reaching goals; it continues with learning from results and adjusting as necessary, thanks to agile approaches and data-driven decision-making. Organizations can maintain focus on their aims and modify their methods for improved outcomes by establishing clear objectives and key results (OKRs). The importance of growth and evolution is emphasized by the concepts of ongoing learning, feedback, and frequent check-ins and updates.

The Entire View:

The insights gained from reading these writings have wider applications in our private life than just the corporate sector. To successfully traverse our own travels, we can put the concepts of data-driven decision-making, adaptability, and continual learning to use. Having the knowledge and perspective to make wise decisions is a great advantage in a world where change is inevitable.

As we come to the end of this examination of these crucial subjects, it's critical to understand that the future is defined by a dedication to making wise decisions, accepting change, and never stopping to learn. In business, personal development, or any other venture they choose, those who can navigate the complex and changing world with agility, data-driven insights, and a collaborative attitude will be well-positioned for success and joy.